MANAGING THE ACADEMIC DEPARTMENT
Cases and Notes

John B. Bennett

American Council on Education • Macmillan Publishing Company
NEW YORK

Collier Macmillan Publishers
LONDON

The American Council on Education/Macmillan Series in Higher Education

Macmillan Publishing Company
A Division of Macmillan, Inc.
866 Third Avenue, New York, N.Y. 10022

Collier Macmillan Canada, Inc.

Library of Congress Catalog Card Number: 83–15860

Printed in the United States of America

printing number
1   2   3   4   5   6   7   8   9   10

Library of Congress Cataloging in Publication Data

Bennett, John B. (John Beecher), 1940-
    Managing the academic department.

    (The American Council on Education/Macmillan series
in higher education)
    Bibliography: p.
    Includes index.
    1. Departmental chairmen (Universities)—United States.
I. American Council on Education.   II. Title.   III. Series.
LB2341.B47   1983   378'.111   83–15860
ISBN 0-02-902650-4

Contents

Foreword

THE POSITION OF DEPARTMENT CHAIRPERSON in the administrative structure of American colleges and universities is just over 100 years old in the more traditional academic disciplines. From the founding of Harvard in 1636 until after the Civil War, the administrative structure of the American college was very simple. In fact, only three events with respect to the evolution of department chairpersons are worth mentioning. The first event was the use of the title dean in 1792, when Samuel Bard was appointed to that post at Columbia University; a new title was needed for the head of the medical college of that institution, and it was decided that there could not be two presidents. The second event occurred when Thomas Jefferson, rector of the University of Virginia, organized six colleges with a professor at the head of each. The third event was the addition of modern languages to the curriculum at Harvard in the 1828–1830 period by Professor George Tichnor and the addition of schools of natural science at Yale and Harvard in 1848—both changes strengthening the academic disciplinary structure which in a few institutions led to the emergence of departments prior to the Civil War.

However, it was not until the advent of the land-grant university at Cornell in 1868, the Harvard administrative reforms of 1870, and the founding of graduate schools at Johns Hopkins and later at Clark University in the period 1876 to 1880 that the department really began to come into its own. The main impetus was for purposes of graduate organizations and student-professor relationships. New departments flourished in the 1880s and in each decade since. The titles of the various disciplinary and subdisciplinary departments, which would fill pages of text, give one a history of the growth and development of the curriculum in our American institutions.

One additional development was the adoption by community colleges after World War II of an organizational system of divisions, headed by a divisional chairperson who often had only limited teaching duties and acted as associate or assistant dean within a group of disciplines. This model was later applied to liberal arts colleges with fairly compact enrollments. Here a model of divisions with or without departments replaced the traditional departmental structure starting in the early 1960s.

Unfortunately, it was not until the last few decades that any attention was paid to the in-service development of faculty members who were selected for the position of department or division chairperson. The first in-service activity was accomplished by some of the scholarly associations, in particular by the Modern Language Association for chairpersons in English, as well as by associations in engineering, accounting, and philosophy. These activities have consisted mainly of summer workshops or special meetings at annual conventions. The focus has usually been on teaching of the discipline, recruitment, quality control, and related matters. In recent years management subjects such as budgeting, mission statement, collective bargaining, and human resources have been added.

Outside of the disciplinary efforts, the first organizational activities for the professional development of department and division chairpersons took place between 1967 and 1971 with three major components. (1) Between 1967 and 1969 a Danforth Foundation grant to the Western Interstate Commission on Higher Education (WICHE), led by David Booth, held six or seven seminars dealing with the role of the department chairperson in the thirteen western states. (2) Between 1968 and 1971, Higher Education Executive Associates (HEEA), a consulting group organized by this writer, developed about twenty seminars at which department chairs were able to meet to discuss their roles and managerial needs. (3) The American Council on Education held two institutes for public institutions in the Midwest, modeled on the HEEA and WICHE activity, under the leadership of Harry Marmion.

The state of the art of these efforts was not spectacular, but some interesting papers emerged which can be seen as classics. These were published in a 1972 book, *The Department Chairman: A Complex Role,* edited by James Brann and Thomas A. Emmet. In 1975 the American Council on Education published the work of Herbert Waltzer of Miami University of Ohio in *The Job of the Academic Department Chairman.* These were the major efforts emphasizing the role and development of department chairpersons prior to 1978.

In 1980 the American Council on Education established the Departmental Leadership Institute; in 1981 it published Allan Tucker's book *Chairing the Academic Department: Leadership among Peers.* Training and development experiences were provided for chairpersons in a number of state systems of universities as well as in several large institutional consortia. Leadership seminars for department and division chairpersons and deans not in state systems were also developed. In addition, well over twenty on-campus workshops for individual institutions and local consortia have been conducted.

This book is the next step in developing materials and activities to assist the professional growth of department and division chairpersons. The author, John B. Bennett, who is a former division head himself, has had considerable experience leading seminars and workshops on the issues that chairpersons face. His scholarly and creative approach in many of these case studies has been tested under his or my leadership with well over 1,000 chairpersons from 1980 to 1983. This set of published cases can contribute significantly to the growth and development of individual chairpersons and can also play a substantial role in workshop experiences.

I urge those who use these materials and Tucker's work as well to follow in our footsteps and to develop further materials and research which will advance the in-service development of department chairpersons so long overdue and so very badly needed. The management expert on Z organization and Japanese business theory, William Ouchi, has suggested in his work that the smallest working unit is the key to quality and productivity in the industrial setting. It is high time we recognized this fact in higher education. Truly, the department chairperson is the key to real institutional vitality. For too long we have ignored this *vital* human resource.

THOMAS A. EMMET
Littleton, Colorado
April 4, 1983

Acknowledgments

SEVERAL OF THE CASE STUDIES in this book have appeared in the "What If?" sections of recent issues (Winter 1982–Spring, 1983) of *Educational Record,* the quarterly of the American Council on Education (ACE), as did a version of Madeleine F. Green's response to "Forward University." In addition, "Early Deadwood" was inspired by "A Tempest in Three Acts," which also appeared in *Educational Record* (Summer 1980). Special thanks is owed to Lois VanderWaerdt, Director of Affirmative Action at the University of Missouri at St. Louis, for her inspiration for "The Handicapped Student."

As in all such efforts, a variety of people contributed to the development of this project in significant but inconspicuous ways. Although such contributions are a natural and inevitable part of human interaction and achievement, it would be unseemly not to mention some special forms of help.

The various respondents to the case studies are to be commended for their willingness to share their perceptions and judgments so publicly. The variety of responses reflects the diversity of leadership styles and institutional settings that are a strength of American higher education.

Among colleagues at the ACE, Jerry W. Miller, Thomas A. Emmet, and James Murray deserve mention for their interest in and support of this project. Jerry Miller went the extra mile in reading and commenting on virtually all of the cases. Special thanks must also go to Laura Jones and Phyllis Goodwin for their work on the word processor.

JOHN B. BENNETT
May 25, 1983
Washington, DC

———————CHAPTER ONE———————

The Academic Department Chairperson

IMPORTANT? Definitely. Overworked? Probably. Prepared for the job? Rarely. This is the typical academic department chairperson. Often almost stumbling into the job, the average chairperson takes quite seriously his or her new responsibilities even if how to meet them has to be learned along the way. Others in the institution can be grateful for this earnestness, because, whether appointed or elected to the job, the chairperson plays a key role in its workings. It is at the department level that the real institutional business gets conducted—it is here that teachers and learners make contact, that researchers find encouragement and direction, and that many of the ways to contribute to the larger community are identified and explored.

The department chairperson is the one responsible for seeing that these things actually get done as they should. As a

1

result, one can argue that the chairperson is crucial in the success of an academic institution. After all, a college or university can lurch along for years with poor administrators at the top. As long as there are good department chairpersons, the integrity of the institution can be maintained. Reverse the situation, however, and watch out!

One would think, therefore, that people would be carefully selected for the job on the basis of managerial experience and aptitude. In fact, of course, chairpersons are typically chosen—whether by colleagues or by deans—for very different reasons. Scholarly accomplishments, regional or national prestige, a pleasant and nonpolitical demeanor, or the "right" political posture—these are the far more customary considerations, together with the occasional judgment that it is an individual's turn for the position or the harsher realization that no one else will take the job.

This is an established tradition and it seems to work, but certainly not because there is logical rigor to it. After all, being a good scholar in graduate school is no guarantee that one will be equally successful as a faculty member. Similarly, being a good teacher or researcher is no guarantee that one will be a good department chairperson. In neither case does the one condition logically entail the other. Nonetheless, the practice at most institutions is to proceed as though there were such connections. Considering the almost ad hoc character of the selection process, it is no small miracle that institutions work as well as they do in these circumstances. The reason must lie with the individual chairpersons and their determination to prevail.

The Nature of the Position

Certainly the job does not come without stress, as the chairperson struggles to cope with the traditional ambiguity of the position. This struggle occurs because the chairperson has always to be looking in two directions, mediating the concerns of the administration to the faculty and vice versa, while at the same time trying to maintain some independent identity and integrity.

The ambiguity of the chairperson's role has both psychological and political dimensions. Psychologically, the position is difficult because it challenges established patterns. Friends and associates can resent the new responsibilities and authority the chair has for their evaluation and curricular assignments. Established relationships are inevitably altered. At the same time that the chairperson has to deal with these challenges from without, he or she is also likely to be troubled by personal identity questions such as, Am I no longer a regular faculty member? Can I escape being tarred or tainted by the administrative connection? Will departmental duties help or hinder my career?

Ambiguity can also mean political precariousness, for both faculty and administration expect loyalty and the chairperson can frequently be smack in the center of conflict. As agent of both sides, the chairperson always runs the risk of alienating one or the other—and occasionally both. Even in less challenging circumstances, some battles simply cannot be won. This may not be at all clear to others. Certainly it is not welcome news, and the chair may suffer the misfortunes of the messenger. Small wonder, then, that the chairperson can often feel alone and regard the demands of the position to be much greater than its rewards.

The position requires that the new chairperson adjust to at least three major and rather abrupt transitions. The first transition is the radical shift from specialist to generalist. As a regular faculty member, one has an area of academic specialization, is hired for it, and is expected to add to it. As chairperson, however, one is required to move from immersion in such individual areas to a much broader understanding of the whole spectrum of pursuits for the department.

This can be a jarring shift, especially in the larger department or in those institutions with divisional structures. As a faculty member, one was trained and socialized to be an authority in and an advocate of a specific area of inquiry. The new chairperson, however, is expected to understand and support the other departmental areas with equal enthusiasm. Competitive intellectual passions that were formerly encouraged are now to be set aside in a new posture of judiciousness. It is a transition that many find difficult. In addition, matters of detail that in one's earlier innocence never arose, suddenly assume great importance.

The new chairperson must learn quickly to apply this fresh judiciousness and breadth of responsibility to curriculum, personnel, and budget. For instance, concerns can quickly balloon about enrollment or staffing patterns in other areas of the department or division that were once of little personal consequence. So, too, the budget figures simply must be wrestled with and memos requesting various plans and justifications must be responded to. In any event, one must become reasonably articulate in these various expressions of the departmental mission. At the same time, most chairpersons do try to continue some activity in their own special academic areas—a challenging effort, involving now difficulties in division of attention as well as of time.

The second shift the chairperson must undergo is from being an individualist to running a collective. Formerly, things could be done pretty much at one's own pace and were subject to significant review only by a few. The individual faculty member would structure the course and its requirements according to his or her own judgment, pursue research in good part according to private interests, and even schedule much of the working day according to personal preference. Students were the main audience, but rarely were they in position to veto. Nor did they require lengthy consultation and persuasion.

As chairperson, one suddenly finds the pace and procedure set by others. No longer can the individual work independently or in isolation. Nothing can be done without at least pondering the necessity or wisdom of consultation. Few things can be done quickly. One must work through others, and they move at their own pace. Credit must be shared too. In fact, if one wishes department approval for an idea, others must be allowed to own it. Sometimes ways must be found for them to propose it. Insisting upon one's own authorship or initiative will not work. A tradition deeply rooted in faculty values has to be set aside.

Personal relationships with department colleagues can also assume an entirely different complexion. Familiar and comfortable working associations will be altered when responsibilities are assumed for annual evaluation, for tenure and promotion recommendations, and for course assignment and scheduling, as well as for such matters as conflict mediation and performance counseling. In addition, many of the faculty members will have unrealistic expectations of the department chairperson, often blaming him or her for events completely outside of the chairperson's control. New problem-solving behaviors have to be learned. Frequently a thick skin must be developed.

These new leadership responsibilities involve demands upon the chairperson that frequently challenge the very aspects that were originally most attractive about higher education as a profession. The traditional freedoms and relative lack of accountability of the faculty member are compromised. The new chairperson must learn to handle with grace the new intrusions upon his or her time and good humor. Resignation is always an option, but it is also clearly a last resort.

The third transition is from loyalty to one's discipline to loyalty to the institution. Earlier I mentioned the need to transcend individual areas of inquiry in order to represent the department or division as a whole. Other faculty members will make this requirement quite clear. The chairperson will also be called upon to transcend the department in order to represent the institution's perspective. Other administrators and circumstances themselves will dictate this requirement.

As institutions confront the increasing financial difficulties ahead, department chairpersons will be given additional burdens. Specifically, they will be expected to manage curriculum and faculty with an eye to what the times permit, not what the discipline should have. Tenure and promotion decisions will become more taxing, for ever-higher standards must be imposed and met. Budget requests will have to be denied. Individual friendships and professional associations will be tested. The conflict between disciplinary and institutional loyalties can be keen and the chairperson will probably be at the center.

Chairpersons will experience these transitions in different ways, of course. Some will find the intellectual tensions to be the challenge. Others will find the personal dimensions the most difficult to bear. Still other problems may be consuming. There will be rewards, too—among them the opportunities to provide curricular direction, to support people and projects of merit, to enjoy additional salary, and to escape suffering under less-competent leadership.

Still, the new chairperson is suddenly thrust into a position requiring considerably different behavior from that he or she practiced as a faculty member. Few institutions provide much by way of recognition of or assistance to the chairperson in coping with these demands. Institutions are well-advised to examine their policies, for the hard times ahead will force increasing reliance upon the chairperson for effective resource management. For that matter, at the end of the chairperson's term, institutions should show their appreciation by helping with the equally abrupt burdens of reentry.

The Role of the Case Study

The case studies that follow are designed to provide one form of assistance to chairpersons, both new and seasoned. Of the three transitions described above, the requirements of running a collective can generate the most practical difficulties. The shift from concentration on individual areas of teaching and research to department concerns is largely a shift in attitude, as is the transition from the context of department to that of the institution. To be sure, these may well be the most difficult adjustments required of a chairperson, and success in making the changes may be the most crucial factor in whether he or she does the job well.

But the practical complexities of administration make their own demands. Even the best and most constructive of attitudes will be insufficient without some strategies for working through typical dilemmas that confront the chairperson. It is toward eliciting some of these strategies and promoting the clearer resolution of some of these dilemmas that the following case studies are devoted. This book is designed primarily for use in discussion formats, but individuals can also profit from its use.

As first-line administrators, more often than not, chairpersons are the key link between the institutional administration and the faculty and students. Whatever they do is hard to undo elsewhere. Despite their importance, however, little attention has been paid to their needs for training and development. As a consequence, there is a need for case studies dealing with department or division chairpersons, heads, or directors. For instance, a review of such obvious sources as Harvard's Institute for Educational Management and the American Council on Education's Institute for College and University Administrators produced only a couple of cases from listings that numbered in the scores. Hence these studies, designed and developed specifically to meet this need.

These materials were originally constructed for ACE's Departmental Leadership Institute (DLI). A number are derived directly from my own experience. Others were inspired by stories I heard while conducting DLI activities. The intent is that the cases will elicit discussion focused on the issues presented. Like all such studies, these rarely admit readily of precise answers. Nor is there necessarily only one correct answer.

The settings provided for the case studies vary. Usually only enough detail is given to illustrate the issues under consideration. More details, I felt, would detract from the common character of the issues—making them problems for chairpersons at liberal arts colleges, say, rather than for those at comprehensive institutions. On the other hand, some effort was spent in evoking a concrete situation and so avoiding the abstractness characteristic of more-analytic presentations.

The issues in the cases are those that with some regularity confront department and division chairpersons, be they in graduate, undergraduate, or community college settings. Naturally there are major differences among these institutions' missions, but the chairpersons will share many of the same basic problems and responsibilities. This is true also of chairpersons in professional schools and colleges.

The unusual strength of the case-study method is the demand it makes upon each individual to analyze problems and to identify and evaluate possible solutions. Rather than passively being led, as he or she would be by an expository narrative, the reader or discussion participant is required to identify the issues. In order to provide the reader with some bases for comparative judgments, responses to the cases presented here were solicited from past and present chairpersons who had participated in DLI activities. These responses display some of the variety that the case-study approach can stimulate.

There are other benefits to the case-study method. When used with a group, this approach provides a common frame of reference for all of the discussants, one in which no single individual is in a privileged position. All have the same information to start with and an equal chance to contribute. Nor is any information privileged; no confidences must be respected, and no one risks being compromised.

In addition, each participant has a chance to test his or her judgments against those of colleagues and to challenge differing positions. Healthy dialogue can only enhance the individual's analytical and evaluative skills. Similarly, this learning environment can be stimulating without being threatening. Everyone stands to gain at least some additional insight and no one will be damaged by outcomes.

In effect, the case-study method reflects the twin assumptions that chairpersons can be resources for one another and that each individual must in the last analysis assume responsibility for his or her own learning. Learning styles differ, but the problem-centered context can be quite effective, drawing as it does on experience and providing the opportunity to sort out the various issues. Above all, it is an active process, one in which the several dimensions of proposed solutions and required interpersonal skills can be identified and explored as each participant desires.

More than cognitive matters are involved, for in addition to the valuable exchange of practices and other information that can occur in issues related to the case studies, participants can work through the feelings of frustration, exasperation, and uncertainty that go with the job. The review of case studies can provide an excellent outlet for these affective dimensions of the position—and the reinforcement that can come with sharing such feelings with others can provide valuable personal insights and yield enhanced self-confidence.

The solitary student of these materials will not enjoy the contributions of colleagues, but other values can accrue. The same opportunity is available for considering how best to respond to quite different situations. The individual can then compare his or her analyses with the responses provided in the book. Whether studied in a group or by oneself, the materials present a risk-free chance for identifying, sorting out, and exploring various administrative options. They provide excellent exercises for developing administrative skills.

Those wishing to lead discussion sessions utilizing these case studies may find some traditional advice to be of help. For instance, initiate the discussion with a question such as, What is going on here? Responses can quickly provide a fairly comprehensive portrait of the issues involved. Discussion can then concentrate on the various options available to the chairperson and their relative merits. Comments can be sought on both the ideal character of the proposed solutions and their practicality or feasibility. Diverse contributions can be elicited by asking whether everyone agrees with one or another observation or suggestion.

Some discussants will be tempted to divert matters by introducing parallel issues in which they have been involved. A certain amount of such sharing can be quite instructive and fruitful, but the discussion leader should be alert to the need to keep the principles at stake in clear view. Sooner or later, depending upon both the particular case study and the discussants, the comments will demonstrate that the relevant dimensions of the case have been exhausted. Sometimes there will be consensus at this point as to the appropriate actions of the chairperson. Not infrequently, however, judgments will be quite diverse, thereby reflecting a diversity of management style and philosophy.

These case studies are to stand by themselves, but they have been developed with an eye toward their possible use with the specific topics of the DLI materials. The chapters that follow group the case studies under various topics dealt with in *Chairing the Academic Department* by Allan Tucker and his associates. Sometimes, however, the issues in a case can just as easily and profitably be discussed under another topic. For instance, many of the issues considered in the studies on performance counseling are also involved in some of the cases on conflict management. Any precise or clear separation is artificial.

The reader will discover few case studies that focus only on faculty evaluation. This is a deliberate feature of the book, for the issues that sometimes make evaluation so difficult are intertwined with those here subsumed under counseling, leadership styles, or conflict.

CHAPTER TWO

Roles, Responsibilities, and Leadership Styles

REGARDLESS OF THE METHOD OF SELECTION, the chairperson is an odd creature and is in an odd spot. Rooted in the faculty like no other administrator but tied to the administration like no other faculty member, he or she has both an excess and a deficiency of identity. As a result, the roles that need to be played are many and the responsibilities can be quite challenging.

Consider, for instance, the position of the chairperson in the context of the issues surrounding the department as the basic academic and institutional unit. Charges against the department are both numerous and long-standing. They include its fostering of undesirable elements of specialism and particularism, the tendency for degree requirements to be established more for the sake of the department than for educational reasons, and the frequent inability of the department to deal with the issue of its own decline. How well, it is asked, can departments deal with the new issues facing higher education when too often they narrow rather than broaden horizons and discourage rather than promote cross-fertilization of ideas? Although the department allows the organization of inquiry in clear centers and structures of learning, these same structures and centers tend almost inevitably to become conservative and to deteriorate into arenas of individual privilege.

These criticisms suggest at least some of the challenges facing the chairperson. For it is the chairperson who with the levers of curriculum, budget, and faculty-staff hiring and evaluation, must work to overcome these problems while at the same time promoting the values that the department's structure embodies. For instance, the chairperson must support both the advance of and the retreat from fragmentation of knowledge. The specialized teaching and research of professors is to be supported, after all, for the department stands to benefit from their work. At the same time, however, isolation between inquiries is to be overcome, boundaries are to be crossed, and new areas of inquiry established. As a result, the chairperson has both to resist and to promote change in curricular and instructional requirements. He or she must learn to weigh, and sometimes to play off, one interest against another—all in the name of promoting both continuity and progress within the department.

The alert chairperson will be aware of the various constituencies with which he or she must deal. The individual department faculty members certainly are the most prominent, though rarely is there any clear unity of thought or value among them. Coalitions may emerge and shift according to the issues. There may also be fairly stable groupings that reflect age, tenure status, or subdiscipline. However, unanimity usually occurs only when other constituencies are threatening.

The college dean and other academic administrators can present such a threat. Certainly they are another major constituency and so claim a good share of the chair's attention and loyalty. But students are a third important group, because it is the chair's responsibility to see that they are adequately served. By the same token, the chairperson has a clear responsibility to the discipline itself, to be sure that the appropriate standards are recognized, set, and indeed met. Groups outside the campus constitute a fifth public or constituency. Some of them are alumni and so perhaps merit identification as a separate group.

Meeting the demands of all of these constituencies would be an impossible agenda. So far as possible, the chairperson must select both the issues and the time in dealing with each group. In that sense the job is certainly political in character. It requires lobbying, negotiating, and building constituent support. Much depends upon the traditions of the department and the institution. It would be a mistake, however, to regard the position as only political.

Ultimately, there is the position of chairperson because within the institution there must be someone tagged as the primary organizational representative of the academic discipline. This individual is charged with creating the one academic department out of the various individual practitioners of the discipline. He or she has to give the discipline its specific institutional shape, texture, and color. And for this, both competence in the discipline and shrewd assessment of individual ability are required.

Certainly each chairperson needs to be clear about the character of his or her authority. Specifically, each chair must recognize the difference between power *over* others that comes from the position itself and power *with* others that comes from one's own personal resources. By the nature of the case in higher education, the latter will usually be far more important than the former. One can issue various directives, but the ability to lead within the department (and indeed within the college or university as a whole) turns far more heavily on leadership style and the uses one can make of such individual personal endowments as charm, intellect, wit, patience—all harnessed to enhance one's persuasiveness.

The case studies in this chapter call our attention to some of the breadth of the chairperson's responsibilities. The cases also suggest the important roles that personal leadership styles can play in meeting some of these challenges. Later chapters will explore such specific issues as dealing with conflict and performance counseling.

A. "Forward University"— The New Department Chairperson

The brand-new department chairperson, especially one coming from outside the institution, is in a particularly vulnerable position. Strength will usually come from longevity, but decisions may have to be made quickly and thereby may threaten a quick demise. In this case study, Isaac Sontag, only two days into the job, finds himself still thinking as a faculty member. His situation requires a different kind of behavior, however. It will no longer do simply to pass along communications from the dean. In fact, to his later consternation, it is just such an act that precipitates Sontag's difficulty. Within a very short time he succeeds in placing himself in a position with excellent chances of alienating his department faculty.

FORWARD UNIVERSITY

A medium-sized denominational university, Forward is located in a rural spot in the Southwest. For many years it has received loyal support from its church constituency. Regardless of whether they themselves were alumni, church members seemed to feel a special relationship to Forward. They encouraged their own children to go there and were especially generous with their contributions and bequests. Forward was able therefore to be selective in its admissions policies and at the same time to attract and retain a good faculty. As a result, the university long enjoyed a reputation throughout most of the Southwest as a "selective" institution and a prestigious one to attend.

The declining birthrate among the church membership, however, recently reduced the size of the college-age church membership. This reduction came at the same time that national demand for cottonseed, the region's chief cash crop, fell off. The impact of these two events on Forward was considerable. Rather than adjusting to a smaller student body, though, the university chose to be less selective in admissions. As a result, faculty members were soon complaining that freshmen were not able to read, write, and calculate at appropriate levels.

It was to this situation that Isaac Sontag recently came as newly appointed chair of the English department. Dr. Sontag brought impeccable academic credentials to this, his first "administrative" position. No stranger to the literature-composition struggle found in many English departments, Sontag believed that good writing skills are best acquired through the study of literature. In fact, it was largely because of the strong literary reputation of Forward's English department that Sontag was so pleased with this new appointment.

While being interviewed for the position, Sontag had inquired specifically about the level of freshman competencies, for he knew that relaxed standards were a problem everywhere. He left the campus with the impression that Forward was still able to be selective and that any problem of reduced student preparation and abilities was small in scope. He had heard of the new Skills Resource Center and believed that it was handling the situation well.

It came as a shock, therefore, when only two days into the job he learned from the college dean that the English department would be required to contribute four rather than two full-time equivalent (FTE) positions to the Skills Resource Center next term. The dean noted in his letter that while the quality of the top-level applicants for Forward had been every bit as high this year as in the past, the number of those in the top rank had shrunk. In order to maintain enrollments at the necessary level, the Admissions Committee had been forced to invite to Forward a larger number of students needing some remedial attention than had been anticipated. Certainly it was higher than at any time in the past. While the dean allowed that this circumstance was unfortunate, he did observe that it provided the student body with greater diversity and gave the faculty an opportunity to experiment with a wider range of instructional techniques.

While weighing how he might respond to the dean, Dr. Sontag decided that the first necessity was to inform his department of this new circumstance. Accordingly, he composed a memo that contained key portions of the dean's letter and requested that the department review the issue at its next meeting, two weeks later. Dr. Sontag was not prepared for the communication he received the next day from a majority of the faculty (twelve out of seventeen). Stating that they were unwilling to support an expanded role for the Center, since it could only operate in a remedial position and thereby lower the standards of the institution, the faculty members urged the chair to "refuse to submit" to the dean's request.

While Dr. Sontag philosophically supported the sentiment of the note and its bias toward literature and against composition, he was uncomfortable as he thought of his responsibilities as chair. On the one hand, he was sympathetic to the twelve, for he knew that as a faculty member he himself would probably have signed the note. One impulse, therefore, was to support them and simply to convey to the dean that the department was unable to comply. He had some ammunition, after all, for the enrollments in the literature classes were stable and the student credit-hour production was adequate—in fact, it was ahead of the university and college average. Perhaps he could get the dean to negotiate downward.

On the other hand, the dean had indicated that four FTE English faculty would be required, not just desirable. And he had made it clear to Dr. Sontag that the university's strict budget constraints prevented the hiring of additional faculty members from outside the university. There was no prospect of any resignations within the department and no personnel slots elsewhere within the university to which Sontag felt he could lay claim.

The situation was particularly troublesome because it was among the twelve who signed the statement that Sontag would have to find the two additional FTE for the Skills Resource Center. Of the five department members who did not sign, one was totally unqualified by temperament and the other four were already significantly involved with the Skills Center. Sontag could not ask them to assume the additional responsibilities. At the very least that would be unfair and create a morale problem. He knew from the files that the previous chair had promised them continued involvement in the literature courses in exchange for partial service to the Center.

None of the twelve had received special training in the

teaching of composition courses, Sontag knew. But he also thought, from talking with colleagues elsewhere and from his reading, that they could make the transition from literature to composition. It would require some extra preparation and there would be additional demands because of the grading burdens. But it could be done.

Sontag keenly felt the need to respond soon to the dean. But he had first to deal with the statement. How should he proceed?

Questions that might be raised include: How successful was Sontag in his interview? What contact should he have had with the dean immediately upon receiving the letter? What contact should he then have initiated with the department faculty? How can Sontag defuse the high feelings among his department colleagues? What kind of long-range planning does the department need and how should he go about starting it? The following two responses touch in very different ways on these and other issues.

Response #1

Chairman Sontag's role falls between the administration and the faculty. He is responsible for communicating the faculty's feelings to the administration on the one hand; on the other, he must interpret and enforce the administration's decisions. This is a classical dilemma for middle-level management people, regardless of profession.

In my opinion, he should call a faculty meeting to let the various members discuss the opposing points of view— perhaps with some prespecified time limits on debate. Then he should acquaint them with reality. The economy has reduced private donations supporting the school. In order to survive, the school has changed its focus from a highly selective to a more open admissions policy. The faculty must adjust or find other employment. The former "academic prestige" will simply not be possible for a number of complex, interlocking reasons. Therefore, one of the services the faculty must now perform is to bring the remedial students to the highest level possible before sending them into a regular program of the department.

Dr. Sontag should make his appointments with regard to seniority, personality, and his best judgment about a person's abilities to teach composition. The professors selected should be given some kind of incentive, as much as the institution's budget allows. The incentive might be financial, or other teaching assignment considerations, or time off. The four FTE could be one class per person of the twelve faculty members, or any number of other divisions and arrangements.

Frankly, I've seen this sort of situation occur at a neighboring college, and I know simply from proximity what a trying experience it can be for the college. But survival depends partly on how well the students are served. If the remedial students are well taught, some will be able to deal with the regular program. If the college is unable and unwilling to deal with the changed character of the student body, it won't have enough students to survive as an institution of learning of any kind. (Brooke Cameron, Department of Art, University of Missouri/Columbia.)

Response #2

After only two days on the job, Sontag instinctively reacts as a faculty member. He knows that the department members, primarily interested in literature, will have great difficulty in accepting the dean's directive and that he, too, would react similarly if he were on the faculty. Yet he must communicate the dean's request to his department and carry it out. This incident has given Sontag a vivid, concrete introduction to the paradoxical role of department chair.

But how has Sontag allowed himself to be trapped in a conflict where the lines have already been drawn and the positions hardened? Sontag made his first mistake when he sent the memorandum to the department. His first stop should have been the dean's office, to learn the background of the directive, to consider his strategies, and to prospect for alternatives. He might have asked the dean the following questions: Why is this need arising? Why did we not know this before? What has been the history of assigning more faculty to the Skills Resource Center? How did the previous chairperson deal with it? What reactions can I anticipate from the department? Sontag might also have used this opportunity to discover what maneuvering room, if any, he had with the dean.

Armed with this knowledge and perhaps some information that would help him anticipate this next phase, Sontag could then turn to the task of communicating the news to the department. His second error consisted of incorporating into his memo portions of the dean's letter. In addressing the entire department, he allowed himself no opportunity for appealing to his colleagues to enlist their cooperation. Instead, he stirred up faculty resentment, which in turn provoked a united opposition against the dean and himself.

If Sontag had not already met individually with members of the English department, now would be the time to do so. Individual conferences would enable Sontag to lay out the problem, solicit suggestions, and perhaps defuse some of the more negative reactions through personal alliances with individual faculty members. If this is a large department, of course, the new chairperson would be unable to meet with all the faculty members in so short a time. But, by the same token, the assignment of two FTE faculty members would not affect a large department as deeply.

Whatever limitations are imposed on institutional communications, the chairperson must accomplish a great deal through department consensus and participation. Thus, good interpersonal relationships with faculty members are a must. Although the chairperson's degree of power varies widely among institutions, he or she always relies heavily on the respect and cooperation of the faculty to run the department.

To be an effective chairperson, Sontag will have to overcome his natural tendency to identify primarily with the faculty. If he does not, his credibility and effectiveness with the administration will be severely undermined. Sontag has to decide which battles are worth waging on behalf of the department, which are not, and which are lost causes. Although Sontag cannot afford to incur the lasting enmity of his faculty at this meeting, he cannot simply join their chorus of protest.

As stated, one of Sontag's earliest mistakes was not doing his homework with the dean. But his first mistake may really have occurred when he took the job. When he accepted the position of chairperson, he knew precious little about the situation he was getting into. With declining abilities of incoming freshmen already a reality on campus, and the Skills Resource Center already geared up to handle the problem, why did Sontag not see the writing on the wall? Did he not ask the right questions when he was interviewed for the position? Quite likely, the dean did not give the job candidates the complete picture of Forward's increasing need for remedial English courses.

Knowing what he did about admission trends at Forward, the dean knew all along the university's need for two additional FTE English instructors for the Resource Center. Yet Sontag did not discover the problem until after he assumed the post and, to make matters worse, he learned about it indirectly, through a letter. Understandably but lamentably, the dean, like many of his colleagues, resorts to the written word to convey bad news. He does not seem to realize that although face-to-face encounters may be painful, they usually generate less residual anger and encourage frank, constructive communication. Written confirmation of a meeting or of news given "for the record" is often necessary and useful, but in serious matters a letter or memo should *supplement* conversation, not *substitute for* it.

Sontag resorted to the same unfortunate measure—a memo—with serious repercussions. Perhaps he can assuage his angry department with explanations and some rewards for the victims of the dean's directive. As the new chairperson, he now faces the first test of his ability to manage conflict. His first step, which already comes too late, should be to open up lines of communication with the members of his department. Sontag will have to mend fences, build personal relationships with his faculty, and summon his powers of persuasion to get on a better footing with the department members and to ameliorate the already difficult situation he has created with his memo. If he does not do this before the department meeting, he will probably find himself taking on the whole faculty at the meeting and being unable to budge them as a group. (Madeleine F. Green, Director, Center for Leadership Development and Academic Administration, American Council on Education.)

This case also draws our attention to the issue of leadership styles. Certainly one issue to explore is the degree to which the chairperson should be aggressive with regard to the dean. For instance, Sontag could go into the dean's office with guns blazing and demand that the dean not put him into such an intolerable position at the very beginning of his tenure at Forward. Alternatively, Sontag could devote all of his efforts to meeting the dean's expectations—without ever challenging the dean or otherwise confronting him. And, of course, there are the various positions between these two extremes.

Leadership styles are also at stake with regard to the faculty members of the department. Certainly Sontag should have learned that how news is presented influences how the faculty will receive it. How, therefore, is Sontag now to fashion and to communicate his vision of the future with respect to his department colleagues? Is it to be rooted in a democratic model, whereby the chairperson simply communicates to others what he or she has determined by poll or other sounding to be the consensus of the department? Or is Sontag to communicate to the department what he is prepared to do in its behalf and to challenge those who would disagree? Is the challenge to be public or private, individual or collective? Clearly there are several options, which collectively are matters of leadership style as much as they are issues of policy or of strategy.

B.   "Summer Session"—The Personal Request

Every manager is faced sooner or later with special requests and appeals. "Summer Session" reminds us of the intensely personal character that the job of department chairperson can assume. The influence one has over the fortunes of colleagues can be a difficult burden to shoulder. Rules can provide help, although rules are also made to be broken.

SUMMER SESSION

Hank Brown was waiting outside the building as his department chair, Sheila Sharp, came out. Sharp had just finished her Friday afternoon class and was looking forward to the weekend. However, she became concerned upon seeing Brown—it was the time of the year to formulate the summer session teaching schedule, and she suspected his eagerness to talk with her might have some connection. It did.

Brown was in a fair state of agitation. It was very important to him, he said, that he teach both of the courses he had submitted to her as part of the summer session offerings. She had not known the details of his personal finances and listened with both attentiveness and embarrassment as he explained the extent of his need. It was clear that he needed all the help he could get. Fortune was indeed fickle, she thought, for it was unjust for Brown's family to be burdened with its present financial loads.

Still, she wished that Brown had not unburdened himself in this way. It almost seemed to be a transfer of loads, for she had not earlier considered his courses to be of especially high priority for the summer session. There were two problems. The first was that one of his courses had been offered the previous summer. Even though the community college drew mainly from a fairly large population of nontraditional students, she doubted that there would be sufficient interest this soon for the course to draw the minimum enrollment. It was true that Brown had not taught it then, but the fact remained that it had been offered.

The second problem was that neither of the courses he was proposing to teach contributed to a balanced curriculum. In formulating the schedule, she always tried to provide both introductory and advanced offerings, as well as both theory and practice courses. It was difficult to provide this balance and also reflect student demand, but she thought it important. The problem now was that Brown's courses would tilt the schedule heavily toward advanced theory courses. Unfortunately, these were the courses he taught best.

On a strictly rotational basis, it was not yet his turn for summer teaching. The college had never been rigid about such matters, however, and student demand and various curricular requirements were generally deemed to take precedence. As chairperson, Sharp had considerable decision-making ability. Still, the faculty paid careful attention to the summer assignments. She certainly did not want to be perceived to be indulging in favoritism, being unfair, or—as the grievance language would have it—making arbitrary and capricious assignments.

Yet her sympathies for Brown were now aroused. He was a good teacher and was faithful in his department responsibilities. Students trusted him, as did his colleagues. He had taken the initiative recently on several curricular issues. In addition, he had volunteered considerable time as faculty advisor to two student groups. She liked to reward such dedication.

But rewards were difficult in a community college setting, and especially one with collective bargaining, where the contract provided for annual salaries to be determined solely by seniority and credentials. The opportunities for encouraging and rewarding initiative and excellence in teaching, as well as general department contributions, were so few in such a situation. She had tried other, nonmonetary, means of encouragement and reward—means such as special letters of appreciation, with carbon copies to the dean and president, and generous praise, both face to face and at department meetings. But she knew that there was nothing like cash to really prove the point.

Assigning Brown the summer school classes was a clear means for Sharp to convey her appreciation. She also knew that this would not be an assignment based on curricular needs. What should be her management policy?

Issues here include: To what degree should a chairperson make management decisions on the basis of individual need rather than department policy? Indeed, what role should individual need play in the development of policies? What is the place of such matters as summer session assignments as rewards for department accomplishments? Suppose Brown had been a close personal friend. What difference would this fact make in your own analysis?

Response #1

To me, Brown's need for extra compensation and his chairperson's desire to acknowledge his good work clearly outweigh the curricular arguments that the summer curriculum should be balanced and that Brown's courses might not draw enough customers. Sharp's decision therefore hinges on the matter of fairness. Is Brown's need to be compensated and rewarded urgent enough to risk arousing resentment in the department?

The answer depends on the department. Sharp must determine whether or not her action would in fact be perceived as "favoritism" and lead to ill feelings on the part of other department members. With the utmost care and sensitivity she should seek to determine the possible effects of assigning Brown to teach out of turn. If she finds that department members are willing to view Brown's case as a justifiable exception to the usual procedure, then Brown's courses could be scheduled. If she finds that some members of the department are likely to resent the situation to the extent that the smooth functioning of the department will be jeopardized, she should decline to schedule Brown's courses.

In any case, Sharp should explain to the agitated Brown that his request is somewhat irregular and she will need some time to consider it. If she eventually has to turn him down, she should make an effort to suggest summer alternatives, such as teaching a section of an elementary survey course at a neighboring institution. (David Browder, Chairman, Department of Mathematics, Simmons College, Boston, Massachusetts.)

This response emphasizes a leadership style based on securing consensus. Department harmony emerges as a basic principle, one that overrides the concern one might have to reward Brown. One might ask, Does fair treatment always have to be equal treatment? Is it unfair to others to treat Brown differently from them?

Response #2

Sheila Sharp is faced with a delicate balancing act: that of trying to respond to the urgent financial needs of Hank Brown while also meeting student demands and curricular requirements. Three basic management approaches are open to her:

1. She can refuse his request by giving department needs and student demand precedence over his personal request.

2. She can allow the two courses to be offered by giving his personal needs priority over department and student needs.

3. She can try to respond to his personal needs while at the same time preserving department priorities.

The following factors must be kept in mind in helping to determine her management policy:

1. It is not Brown's turn to teach summer school; however, the college has never been rigid about adhering to a strict rotational system.

2. The courses he is proposing are not needed and would throw departmental offerings off balance.

3. Brown is worthy of being rewarded.

4. Sharp has considerable decision-making ability, but she does not want to be accused of making arbitrary or capricious assignments.

With the above considerations in mind, I would recommend approach #3, which could be effected in several possible ways:

- The most desirable option would be to ask Brown to change the proposed courses to either one or two practically-oriented ones, depending on the overall offerings in the department. It is not wise to leave the theory courses in the schedule if the matter can be worked out otherwise.

- If the new courses cause a conflict with another teacher's offerings, Sharp can appeal to the teacher to allow Brown to replace him or her this summer as a special consideration, with the agreement that the favor would be returned sometime in the future. This option is less desirable than the preceding one because it involves another party.

- If an adjustment in course offerings is not feasible, Sharp might represent the case to the dean or to some other administrative official. Occasionally, there are special summer projects, academic and nonacademic, for which teachers receive remuneration. (This may not be a viable option in the community college setting, but it could be pursued if it is.)

I believe it is important that Sharp *try* to respond to Brown's request but without sacrificing or compromising department standards or the needs of students and other teachers. If the above proposed solutions or others are feasible, she should use the one that best applies. If there is no possible way to accommodate him, then, regretfully, I believe it is her responsibility not to approve the two proposed courses. (Brother Vincent Malham, Chairperson, Liberal Arts Division, Christian Brothers College, Memphis, Tennessee.)

C. "Robin Strong"—The Token Chairperson

The chairperson who represents a threat to established department attitudes and values is one figure on the scene. The problems such a threat creates can be quite difficult to handle. Consider the plight of Robin Strong, who is facing a challenge to her authority from some of her department members.

ROBIN STRONG

Dr. Robin Strong was chair of the mechanical engineering department at the Wyoming Institute of Technology, a public, technology-oriented institution. She was the only woman chairperson in an institution with a vast preponderance of male administrators, faculty members, and students.

Although recent years had brought an increase in the number of women engineering students, Dr. Strong confessed to close friends that she still felt uncomfortable. As the "token" woman chairperson, she carried all the burdens of those in such a position: undue demands upon her time to provide counseling for women students, requests to speak before a wide range of community groups wanting the perspective of the female engineer, and heavy committee responsibilities where her role was to provide gender representation.

In addition to these burdens, she had to cope with the suspicion that a woman meets in a profession that has always been almost exclusively male. "Where does your husband teach?" was a common question at the professional meetings. "How come you're so good at math?" was a frequent line at cocktail parties. Some of these remarks were undoubtedly intended as complimentary, she knew, and were merely clumsily phrased or delivered. Other comments were more blunt, and even the most generous interpretation could not ignore a hostile, sexist edge. The previous chair was especially adept in speech richly colored with sexual overtone and innuendo.

Fortunately, he had retired the previous year, and the corridor and committee conversation was now less blatantly macho.

The environment remained difficult, though, and Strong was quite convinced that it was indeed only affirmative-action pressures on the institute that had led to her appointment as chair. The department accepted her appointment, but it was not a warm reception and there was no honeymoon. Had there been an election, she often reflected, she would never have become chair, despite her credentials, which she knew were good.

As it was, her colleagues seemed caught between what she intrepreted as their distaste for a woman supervisor and their traditional respect for the hierarchy and its decision-making authority and prerogatives. Strong knew that several of her department colleagues had dearly wanted the appointment themselves. After her selection they, for the most part, were rather distant and displayed a less-than-enthusiastic attitude toward department responsibilities.

Her work outside the department had equal challenges. For instance, she at one time had looked forward to being on the dean's Academic Council. However, as a council member, she found that her contributions were either outright ignored or politely received with no follow-up. In fact, she had never found reference in the council minutes to anything important she had said.

Overall, the position was a lonely one, and the monetary rewards insufficient. In fact, if it were not such a clear statement of failure, Robin would have resigned. The latest flap certainly revived such thoughts. The problems with the evaluation process seemed to be the last straw. The senior members of the department had begun undercutting her authority by refusing to take seriously the new evaluation efforts, bringing her right to the edge of cold, clear anger.

A year earlier, Strong had worked with a department committee to establish a new faculty-evaluation system. At the suggestion (indeed, the insistence) of the junior faculty, the use of student evaluation forms was mandated, as were provisions for annual visitations by both peers and the department chairperson. Despite some grumbling at the department meeting, the policy was adopted.

Now, however, several of the senior faculty were resisting the new procedures. Somehow they would always overlook distributing the evaluation forms. And when it was time to schedule a classroom visitation they would procrastinate and demur, claiming privileges of rank and of tenure. One objected that he had been there twenty years and surely had established his teaching competence. It is important to evaluate the new and inexperienced faculty members, he said, but it is a waste of everyone's time to review the tenured people. Another senior professor indicated that the department had functioned well before, without this kind of "mothering," and that he for one saw no reason to change now.

Robin felt that this was simply outrageous behavior and that the disagreement raised fundamental issues both of equity and of resource management. How should she proceed at this point? What stategies can you identify that will help?

The following responses to this case are interesting for the perspectives they display. The first analyzes the problem with no reference to the difficulties Strong feels as a token chairperson. The second response, however, regards these felt difficulties as part of the problem, indicating a sexist attitude on Strong's own part.

Response #1

Robin Strong knows she cannot *make* anyone among her faculty do anything if the faculty member does not want to do it. She can, however, establish a basis for her own actions and, with that clearly detailed for her faculty, function with or without those senior members who do not wish to participate in evaluations of their teaching.

For example, she can say simply that she has been called upon by the department committee to institute evaluation procedures. She can invite everyone to participate and in so doing can remind them all that as part of her own responsibility for evaluation she will mention, among other things, their teaching competence. Since she will have no evidence to go on but that gathered by student and peer—and her own—evaluations, she will be forced to point out in the cases of those who do not participate that, because of their reluctance, she cannot say anything at all about their teaching.

If publications and service are both evaluated and teaching is explicitly not, those faculty who do not cooperate will be clearly left in at least an awkward position, and more than likely in a position that will deny them merit increases on the basis that there is no evidence one way or the other about the quality of their teaching. Some may never come around; that makes distribution of the usually rare merit raises that much easier. (John H. Irsfeld, Department of English, University of Nevada/Las Vegas.)

Response #2

Poor Dr. Strong! With such a name, she is probably never able to cry, or be tired, or lose a game, or be a follower! Her paranoia and self-doubt have made her professionally defensive and socially severe. She's supersensitive and sexist!

Robin! Stop being such a bird! Relax and enjoy your appointment, relax with the exchange available as you engage in small groups with women. And if your contributions to meetings aren't noted in the minutes, move that they be amended to include them! When you say no, be positively clear about it!

Robin, just an appointment ago you participated with your peers in voting some constructive changes in evaluation styles in your department. Continue to participate with your peers in facilitating the procedure. Form small groups and evaluate one another. Invite another group to evaluate you. Propose that your twenty-year experts demonstrate their favorite techniques for other department members. Perhaps they'd allow a class to be videotaped! Perhaps they'd conduct a faculty workshop and so share some of their favorite lectures. Perhaps senior members would pair with junior members to discuss a variety of ways to present new material. Perhaps faculty would meet to devise a student survey—or maybe they'd invite students to develop and evaluate criteria by which they'd wish to be evaluated.

Tapes and studies from other institutions could become the subject of department meetings. Perhaps visitations or conferences could be financed by the institute. Course development could be encouraged by financial reward or released time.

Robin, it's time to sing a new song. Cheer up! (Marilyn Watt, Chair, Communications Department, Canisius College, Buffalo, New York.)

D. "Claudius"—Dealing With the Dean

Dealing with evaluation issues and relating to the dean are major responsibilities of every chairperson. This case study deals with both responsibilities.

"Claudius" presents a particularly challenging promotion decision for the chairperson, a challenge stemming from a reduction in institutional finances. In addition to weighing the relative merits of two associate professors and considering the importance that should be attached to affirmative-action considerations, the chairperson must also decide what approach to take with the dean. This study raises questions of leadership style as well as of responsibilities of the position.

<hr/>

CLAUDIUS

Last week the dean made it very clear to Claudius that institutional circumstances permitted consideration of only one promotion to full professor within the department this year. The university had a long-standing policy against "honorary promotions." Advancement in rank was to come only after exhaustive review. And each promotion was to be accompanied by a base salary increment of at least $2,000. Given this university policy, the current financial difficulties meant that the number of promotions had to be severely restricted.

At this moment, however, Claudius was wishing that the dean had said simply that no promotions could be given. Certainly that would have simplified matters, for within the department there were two outstanding associate professors, both of whom were eligible this year for promotion.

One, Jill Springer, had just received notice from a major university press that the manuscript for what would be her second book had been accepted for publication. Her research had already been noticed by others and she was becoming a recognized figure in her area. In addition to being an excellent scholar, she had established quite a favorable reputation as a teacher. Both majors and students outside the department flocked to her classes. Her student evaluations were uniformly impressive.

The other, Ricardo Gonzalez, also enjoyed a reputation as an excellent teacher—a reputation certainly supported by the student evaluations. In fact, Claudius had often heard superlative comments about Gonzalez from both students and department members. Although Gonzalez had not published as much as Springer, his output was certainly adequate—far more, in fact, than most of the full professors in the department. He had also given generously of his time to committee work and to student advising, and, unlike Springer, was active in the national professional organization.

The two were clearly different personalities and had correspondingly different professional strengths. One had a more disciplined mind, but it could border on pedantry. The other was more intellectually curious, but also given more to general synthesis than to clear focus. However, Claudius was unable to differentiate significantly between their accomplishments and their value to the department.

Within both the department and the university women were underrepresented, and at the upper faculty ranks they were particularly scarce. Underrepresentation of Hispanics was even more glaring, but Claudius felt uncomfortable in making that a key factor in a promotion recommendation.

The department tenure and promotion committee had been absolutely no help. The members had recommended both associate professors with equal enthusiasm. When Claudius requested a clearer reading in light of the dean's statement, the committee said it was simply unable to recommend one over the other.

After receiving the committee's report, Claudius pondered

making a similar statement to the dean. Talent was not evenly distributed among departments, after all, and promotion policies should be flexible enough to reflect this fact. On the other hand, while the dean had indicated that she expected the chairpersons to exercise independent judgment, Claudius was concerned about appearing indecisive in choosing between the two. And if he pushed for both, it was possible that neither promotion would be supported and that the department would get a black eye to boot.

Are there other factors that Claudius should weigh in evaluating Springer and Gonzalez? What strategies should he adopt with the dean? How aggressive should he be in seeking an exception to the conditions she has presented?

The ambiguity of the department chairperson's role presents itself in many ways, but here it is manifest in the question, Is the department chairperson to view himself or herself as advocate primarily of the department members or of the institution? Very different strategies are suggested in the answers to this question.

Response #1

The center of this case seems to me to be the relationship between the chairman and the dean. That is, the dean's reaction to a double recommendation will depend partly on her respect for and trust in the chairman. Is the department a strong one? Does its tenure committee carry weight? Does the chairman have a history of indecisiveness? There is also the question of the dean's own preference—particularly on the minority issue, which is more her responsibility than the chairman's. It may be, for example, that minority representation is exactly the argument that would lead the dean to go along with both promotions. In other words, if a decision on merit really is impossible, the chairman probably has to take on his least favorite role: that of politician.

Assuming a "usual" situation (the department is neither outstanding nor weak, etc), the chairman needs to discuss with the two people which of them can most easily defer promotion a year (a key phrase is "this year" in the first sentence of the case). If no accord is reached he will have to flip a coin. Either way, his recommendation is likely to read, "Both are qualified, but if only one can be chosen I recommend X this year and Y the next." (Charles W. Crupi, Department of English, Albion College, Albion, Michigan.)

Crupi's response rightly suggests the importance of the personal relationship between the chairperson and the dean. Formal job descriptions simply set the stage for the chairperson, and what he or she is actually able to accomplish depends on the degree of trust already established. Similar comments about the department itself are in order. Incidentally, one possibility not mentioned is for Claudius to defer both promotions until next year—thereby avoiding the feelings that could arise if only one is promoted this year. Consider the following, rather different, response:

Response #2

Claudius should prepare and forward materials to the dean concerning his recommendation that both Jill Springer and Ricardo Gonzalez be promoted to the rank of professor this year.

In his letter of transmittal, Claudius should make clear his understanding of the dean's statement that because of the limited amount of funds available for salary increments, only one promotion to full professor per department would be considered this year. He should then state his belief that as a department chairman he is responsible for forwarding to the dean for review at the college level, the credentials of *all* candidates for promotion to full professor who have been deemed worthy of such promotion by the department tenure and promotion committee and the department chair.

Claudius should assure the dean that he recognizes it will be difficult to distinguish selectively among individuals from different departments at the college level on the basis of the relative merit of their professional accomplishments. He should then state his opinion that, in spite of these difficulties, such action is preferable to awarding salary increases to individuals according to the assignment of funds to departments on a quota (one per department) basis. Claudius should express his concern that an inflexible promotion policy may well result in spreading the promotion salary increases broadly and indiscriminantly across the college. And he may wish to add that he is sure the dean would not want this to happen.

Claudius should then proceed to assure the dean that in recommending both Springer and Gonzalez for promotion, more than normal selectivity has been observed at the department level and that every effort has been made to distinguish between the relative merit of each one's professional activities. He should provide detailed information concerning the rigorous review process that the department tenure and promotion committee followed in its deliberations concerning Springer's and Gonzalez' candidacies for promotion. He should state the following in regard to both Springer and Gonzalez:

1. There is clear evidence of a sustained and distinguished record of research, the high quality of which has been confirmed in written statements provided by off-campus peers.

2. There is a substantial and unequivocal record of excellence in teaching confirmed by confidential statements from students and colleagues in the department.

3. There is a satisfactory record of service.

Claudius should then emphasize that in his department teaching represents the faculty member's most important responsibility, and that his evaluation of the quality of Springer's and Gonzalez' activities in this area confirms the conclusion reached by the department tenure and promotion committee—that their work is excellent. He should also state that both candidates have pursued research appropriate to their responsibilities in the department, and that he considers the quality of these efforts to be excellent, as did their peers off campus. Finally, he should make it clear that no amount of service in the department can compensate for a lack of skill in teaching or research, and that while all faculty members in the department are expected to render a reasonable amount of service, as has been the case with Springer and Gonzalez, this is clearly subordinate to the other two categories of activities —teaching and research.

Claudius should end his letter with a statement that although it has not been possible to differentiate between Springer and Gonzalez at the department level, in so far as the quality of their professional accomplishments is concerned, he believes such selective discrimination can be made at the college level concerning their accomplishments as compared with those of faculty members in other departments.

It might be helpful for Claudius to request a meeting with the dean to discuss this recommendation.

If the criteria established at the department level for promotion to the rank of professor are consistent with those at the college level, if the review process has been conducted properly, and, if the candidates are indeed equally qualified for promotion as Claudius and the members of the department tenure and promotion committee believe them to be, both Springer and Gonzalez should be approved for promotion at the college level. If the dean is adamantly opposed to modifying the policy of limiting promotions to one per department, the college tenure and promotion committee members will have to try to make a choice between Springer and Gonzalez. They will probably decide to award the promotion to Springer because her publication record appears to be more impressive. However, if neither of the candidates is promoted—as Claudius fears might be the case because he recommended both of them—this says a great deal about the review process at the college level. This is simply a chance he will have to take. (Donald E. McGlothlin, Chairman, Department of Music, University of Missouri/Columbia.)

E. "Consulting"—Distributing Departmental Burdens

Let us turn to another challenge that the chairperson can face with regard to leadership roles and styles. It is rather obvious that the chairperson should know the various strongpoints of department members. Certainly the judicious use of faculty resources within the department can hardly occur if the chairperson does not understand different individual competencies and projects, among them consulting activities. Such consulting involvements by faculty are widely considered to contribute to faculty expertise and talent, augmenting the strengths that can be brought to the classroom and to student advising. However, they also present a significant opportunity for individual abuse.

The case study "Consulting" illustrates some of the issues that can arise in this area. Quality University is not unusual for having a vague consulting policy—much latitude is often left to the individual faculty member.

CONSULTING

Flora Green is in her first year as chairperson of the agricultural economics department at Quality University. There are nineteen full-time faculty members in the department and, although the university is not a land-grant institution, the College of Agriculture does have a good reputation. The state is a large one and the land-grant university is at the western end of it. Consequently, people in the eastern region of the state frequently look to faculty at Quality for leadership and assistance in agricultural issues.

Excited about her new position, Flora had often felt that she had administrative abilities. Apparently others agreed, because, as she had later learned, she had been the search committee's first choice, over even a very strong inside candidate. It was well that she had really wanted the job, she reflected, for the whole difficult mess about consulting presented a real challenge.

The university policy stipulated only that faculty could spend an average of one day per week in consulting activities. Nowhere was there any indication as to how many days could be taken at a time, whether weekends were included or excluded, or whether travel was to be counted or not. As a result, there was no uniformity of interpretation within the department, people were confused about what was appropriate and what was permissible, and there was complete unclarity on the relationship of consulting to service and to salary increase.

Some faculty members were apparently spending a good deal of their time consulting for regional industries and rarely seemed to be on campus or in the office. Flora had already heard some grumbling among students about two professors in particular. She visited with one of them, Fred Fastbucks, simply to find out, as she told him, what activities he was busy with. Fastbucks was somewhat evasive about the extent of his consulting activities but was emphatic in stressing the importance to the department of professional activities outside the university.

Flora had no quarrel with the concept itself. Consulting, she knew, is an excellent way of adding to a professor's understanding of his or her field. Book learning alone is inadequate. Many research projects, she suspected, had been conceived in consulting activities. She knew the department profited in other ways, too: contacts in the field usually meant internships for students and placement possibilities later on for graduates. And it was not unknown for a university to acquire valuable equipment or even grants from industries whose first contact with the institution had been through the work of a faculty consultant. Of course, consulting was also an important source of additional income for faculty members.

Still, it was clear to her that consulting should be undertaken to supplement, not take the place of, a professor's normal teaching, research, and service involvements. One problem she had clarified for herself as a result of talking with Fastbucks was the matter of records. The normal practice was for faculty members to file a brief report at the end of each semester, indicating the extent of their consulting activities. There was no way she could figure out the real extent of someone's activities simply by reading that he or she had spent eighteen days in the past eighteen weeks consulting for three different companies. (Did this include travel time? Weekends? Was it eighteen days in a row?) Yet she was not at all eager to request additional reporting procedures from the faculty. She knew what a fuss that would create!

Flora had already been visited by a couple of the more conscientious department members, who had referred obliquely to the need for everyone to pull his full share in student advising and committee work. It was clear that the department chores were not being distributed or shared equally. The issue of equity was a difficult one, moreover, as the "big gun" of the department made no secret of his own extensive activities off campus.

The only member of the department who had a national reputation, John Brightlight, seemed always to be someplace else. Students in his courses complained that, more often than not, faculty members other than Brightlight conducted his classes. This was obviously unsatisfactory. On the other hand, the department needed him, probably more than he needed it. It was quite helpful to the department in its research activities as well as its status generally to have a luminary of his stature. Flora did not want to cross him.

The degree to which paid consulting should count as part of one's service responsibilities was another touchy issue. Those who were most conscientious about department duties seemed also to be the ones most likely to contribute their services to professional associations and regional agencies. These faculty members, when it came to merit determination for salary awards, were not enthusiastic about awarding people like Fastbucks twice—particularly when he was rumored to be paid so lucratively.

A final, related, issue Flora knew she had to confront and resolve was presented by Jim Dolittle. A full professor who had been with the university twenty-three years, Dolittle had recently invested in a feed store in a neighboring town. He was spending increasing amounts of time analyzing and supervising operations there and was frequently not available to students. Flora herself had dropped by his office fruitlessly three times in a row. The fourth time she asked him directly about his off-campus activities. He responded that his work with the feed store was really a form of consulting and so he was doing nothing different from department colleagues.

What strategies should Flora adopt to deal with these issues?

Establishing a fair departmental practice can be challenging, especially when the faculty's interest and activity in consulting varies widely. Certainly one must feel sympathetic with those faculty members who are pulling more than their share of time-consuming department chores.

This case also illustrates the difficulties that can come from having a luminary within the department. The rules defining the conditions under which others labor have to be adjusted. Inevitably, procedural exceptions seem to be made, or special policies created. The chairperson is in a difficult position when required to refuse to grant such exceptions and lacks ordinary forms of leverage—unless he or she is prepared for the luminary to leave when the line is drawn.

Two other issues in the case deserve note. One is the allocation of merit-salary increases in a fashion that reflects direct contributions to the department. How is one to distribute such funds fairly, recognizing the quite uneven financial returns between those with heavy consulting schedules and those who spend more time in campus activities? The other issue is the difference between working in one's own business and working as a consultant. After all, Jim Dolittle can claim that he is performing for some of his clients precisely the same services that colleagues might provide as consultants to others.

Response #1

The role of consulting in an academic department varies greatly across the disciplines within the university. It is, or at least should be, more important in the "professional" disciplines than in the traditional liberal arts areas; the sciences are increasingly assuming a more professional, as opposed to a purely academic, role with a concurrent increase in the importance of consulting.

Even within the professional disciplines, consulting should not become the predominant activity for faculty members. The amount of time devoted to consulting should be limited, and it should be scheduled so as to minimize interference with normal academic responsibilities, particularly teaching and work with students. Rather than rely on an arbitrarily determined standard of X number of days per week or month, academic units should focus on the extent to which consulting actually interferes with the faculty member meeting his or her responsibilities. Consulting activities limited to weekends and/or times when they do not interfere with normal academic responsibilities need not be restricted except when they begin to reduce the faculty member's effectiveness as measured by evaluations of classroom performance, research productivity, and service activities.

A properly structured reward system is important in determining the role of consulting in an individual faculty member's activities. In a professional discipline, consulting should be included in the activities evaluated in determining pay, promotion, and tenure. However, consulting is an additional activity and not a replacement for the traditional trinity of teaching, research, and service. As such, it should carry a relatively small weight in the evaluation process; a range of 10 to 25 percent for weights is appropriate.

How consulting is to be assessed is a crucial factor in the evaluation process. Routine, repetitive activity should receive only light consideration, since it represents activity undertaken primarily for remuneration and is unlikely either to add significantly to the faculty member's "real-world" knowledge or to produce research ideas. Consulting activities in new areas or involving new problems, on the other hand, can produce both and should be rewarded within the limitations set forth above. Running a business "on the side" does not qualify as the latter type of consulting.

By allowing and rewarding consulting on a limited basis, an academic unit can encourage faculty to consult and achieve the benefits ascribed to consulting without tilting the scales too heavily toward it. Because of the low weight assigned to consulting, an active consultant who neglects or minimizes his or her responsibilities in the more traditional areas will fare relatively poorly if colleagues are working at teaching, research, and service.

Based on the discussion above, Flora should take several steps:

1. She should inform the faculty that while consulting will be considered in evaluations, it will not be heavily weighed and that routine repetitive consulting will receive little credit. She should clearly state that running a business "on the side" is, at best, equal to routine repetitive consulting. An obvious result of considering consulting in the evaluations is a requirement that such activity be reported in some detail with regard to the type of work done and the time committed.

2. She should point out to the active consultants that unless they meet their responsibilities in the areas of teaching, research, and service they can expect to fare poorly in the evaluation process.

3. She should work with the active consultants in arranging teaching and advising schedules that will allow a "reasonable" amount of consulting with minimum conflict between department and outside activities.

4. If a faculty member insists on an excessive amount of consulting, she should suggest a reduction in his or her appointment to less than 100 percent. This would allow the faculty member to maintain his or her consulting load while reducing his or her commitment to and salary from the institution. (Michael C. Walker, Head, Finance, Insurance, Real Estate and Law, North Texas State University, Denton, Texas.)

Response #2

Consulting policy is one of the most politically sensitive topics to be found in academia. Particularly in state institutions, administrators often believe the less said about consulting the better, because public and legislative opinion is too easily aroused against prevailing norms for faculty consulting activities.

A chairperson desiring to deal with abuses of consulting privileges would encounter substantial resistance to any effort to create new policy guidelines at the department level until the university as a whole becomes committed to formulating a clear policy statement. Through discreet inquiries among other chairpersons and higher administrators, a single chairperson can often set in motion such a university-level effort, preferably through the mechanism of a faculty committee.

Once the matter becomes a topic of institutional concern, individual departments become motivated to address the topic on their own. A wise chairperson might then ask for volunteers within the department to develop department policy guidelines that speak to the particular contingencies of their discipline—opportunities, existing practices, and so on. The rationale for working on a parallel basis with a university-wide committee would be to ensure the latter's familiarity with models appropriate to particular departments. In constituting a departmental committee to work on this problem, the chairperson should select one or two faculty members aware of the need for better consulting policy and whose own careers reflect a reasonable and defensible balance of professional activities, including paid consulting.

To assist the department committee in its work, the chair might offer to write to a selected set of comparable institutions and request copies of consulting-policy documentation already developed on these campuses.

Such a strategy for dealing with consulting problems, while hardly free of risk and potential error, is most likely to produce useful results by virtue of the extensive involvement of the faculty in policy formulation.

Let's face it—no amount of policy documentation, however carefully conceived, however fair, however well written, will ever take the place of voluntary compliance with well-understood but *implicit* norms based on good professional judgment. There will always be a few who abuse a good thing, but it is a mistake to write a policy for these persons. In developing policy guidelines of an explicit nature, it is probably wiser to err in the direction of less specificity rather than more. The chairperson's public acknowledgement of this principle would serve to reduce the apprehensions of conscientious faculty members about participating in the development of guidelines. (David

R. Seibert, Department of Speech and Theatre, University of Nevada/Reno.)

The department chairperson has many roles to play and a variety of leadership styles from which to chose—although undoubtedly one will be his or her primary style. Among the challenges to be faced will be fashioning the direction of the department, determining the appropriate distribution of available burdens and resources, and coping somehow with the inevitable paper work. In addition, he or she will have to deal with conflict, unsatisfactory performance, and the myriad unsettling problems that go with the job. The following chapters will explore some of these.

--------- CHAPTER THREE ---------

Dealing with Conflict

FACULTY MEMBERS are notoriously individualistic. Each faculty member prefers to go his or her way—on course construction, text selection, student evaluation, and research projects. Each cites the demands of professional judgment in justification. Sometimes this radical individualism is augmented by large egos and professional jealousies. As a consequence, it is inevitable that conflicts between faculty will arise. They are the natural outcome when two or more free agents must work together.

The presence of conflict is not necessarily negative. It need not, for instance, reflect individual behavioral deficiencies. Nor does its presence mean that the institution is mismanaged. In fact, conflict can play an important role in developing creative responses to new situations and circumstances. There is a dialectic in the development of organizations as well as of ideas. Disagreement is the springboard for new directions. Complete unanimity of judgment or identity of practice and behavior is a sign of decay, not of vitality.

Still, conflict can be excessive and can issue in destructive confrontation and hostility. This negative form of conflict will concern us in this chapter, for it is just such negativeness that the chair must try somehow to avert or resolve. Once aroused, enmity can linger and sometimes spread into other areas and activities. It can quickly reverse previous departmental gains and threaten future prospects.

Such negative conflict can stem from differences in personal values. Political and social philosophies, for instance, can be at odds—as in the case of differing individual assessments of collective bargaining or of liberal education. Sometimes the conflict is rooted in different sources of information, as when the facts about some issue are not fully disclosed. Certainly such communication failures can aggravate existing conflicts. And, since there is never enough time, space, or money, there is perennial competition for these resources.

Some conflicts will be between faculty members in a situation that permits only one course of action, as when departmental and curricular priorities are in dispute, or when evaluatory judgments clash, or when burdens or rewards seem unevenly distributed. Other conflicts stem from student-faculty disagreements, disputes with other departments, or even from department-college challenges. Throughout, the chair is thrust into the middle and faced with the need to mediate, negotiate, resolve. Of course, sometimes it is the chairperson who is clearly at one end of the conflict.

Conflict resolution, however, is rarely learned at graduate school. Fortunately, some people are by disposition natural mediators. They seem to know intuitively how to reduce tension and how to create alternatives acceptable to all. But even these individuals face an imposing challenge as chairpersons. And others just have to work harder in developing their skills. The institution is not always a help. Although chairpersons have responsibility for conflict resolution, any institutional authority to do so may well be so resented that it exacerbates the problem. As a result, it can take substantial personal resourcefulness to heal genuine divisions among peers.

It is important to be aware of problems likely to accelerate the conflict and to avoid them or to diminish their prominence. Similarly, a wise chairperson will hunt for ways to reduce the level of emotional and personal investment that parties to the conflict have at stake. Such tactics can minimize the level of damage, but strategies must still be developed to resolve the problem or to isolate it. The following case studies illustrate some of the conflicts chairpersons can face. Both immediate tactics and broader strategies are at issue.

A. "Faculty Lifestyles"—Dealing with the Students

There can be a fine line between the outspoken and the dogmatic faculty member. Both can generate student protest and both will cite the protection of academic freedom. Only the former deserves this protection, however, and it can fall to the chairperson to distinguish between them. The following case presents a clear case of conflict between faculty member and student, conflict that is brought directly to the department chairperson for resolution. The issue concerns the course material and whether it is being presented in an outspoken or a dogmatic fashion.

FACULTY LIFESTYLES

Calvina Short was in her second year as chair of the political science department at a fairly prestigious, independent liberal arts college in the South. She enjoyed her academic discipline and her administrative responsibilities. She had been able to keep up her research, and her duties as chair of the seven-member department were not demanding.

In fact, she had just been congratulating herself on her good fortune, when an agitated sophomore entered her office. Mike Straight had requested the appointment the previous day without indicating the reason. Because the student was talking quite fast today, it took Dr. Short a while to discern the problem.

As she listened it became clear that Dr. Sappho was the

problem. An assistant professor with a doctorate from an Ivy League college, Dr. Sappho had come with a reputation as a promising political scientist and an aggressive feminist. Dr. Short had felt pleased at recruiting her the previous spring, for the chair felt that diversity of views was healthy, particularly at an institution in a fairly conservative region.

Mike had no quarrel, he said, with the value of a diversity of viewpoints. He had learned much from Sappho, and he was sure that others in the class in contemporary political theory had as well. It was good for them, he thought, to be forced to grapple with issues such as the ERA and equal pay for equal work. In fact, he had changed his mind on many issues.

What rankled, however, was the way Dr. Sappho seemed to be pushing her particular lifestyle. She appeared to go out of her way to challenge traditional positions. Mike recounted the time Sappho had spent the whole class period arguing that the state discriminated against individual rights when it granted special status, as well as legal and tax benefits, only to heterosexual couples.

Mike said he thought it just not right to crusade in the classroom for or against lesbianism or any other sexual behavior. He had spoken of this to Dr. Sappho, he continued, but with no success. The professor had responded that it was just such "academic neutralism" that was responsible for the repression of people everywhere. She had made her point with strong language—the sort ordinarily reserved for the locker room.

It was not just he who was upset, Mike added. The women in the class were particularly offended and were talking about having their parents write to the college president. Mike, however, had thought that Dr. Short should be told about the problem first. What, he asked, did she plan to do about it?

The conflict here revolves around the classroom posture of the instructor. It could also be illustrated by the professor as an outspoken Marxist or activist environmentalist. In each of these cases ideology can play a major role and the faculty member involved can cite academic freedom as justification. The present case is different only in that it includes a special and sensitive personal element that heightens the difficulty involved.

Surely no chairperson would care to deny academic freedom. On the other hand, such freedom is no license to proselytize, to use the lectern as a pulpit, or to violate accepted standards of curricular or instructional balance. Such charges must be based on reliable information, however, and in "Faculty Lifestyles" the chairperson has first to gather appropriate evidence in order to determine what, in fact, is occurring.

Suppose the professor is consistently taking controversial stands as a deliberate instructional tactic. Would this circumstance justify the uproar she seems to be creating? Should the chairperson then counsel the professor that his or her pedagogy is failing and for that reason should be immediately changed? Suppose, however, that the instructor also truly believes what he or she is telling the class. Would this be significant? Must a good instructor avoid commenting on issues about which he or she feels strongly? If it is a matter of degree, how is the line to be determined?

Other questions that might be raised include the following: What immediate response or responses should be made to the student? How should the issue be presented to the faculty member? What about the charge that the professor uses coarse and offensive language? What sort of investigation, if any, is appropriate? Since the professor is untenured, should the chairperson counsel her that stridency and vehemence in either pedagogy or idealogy is a poor way to secure a favorable tenure vote? Could such "pragmatic counseling" turn out to be a mistake if there were later to be a suit over a denial of tenure? What, if anything, should Short do to alert the president to the potential problem?

Consider the following two responses.

Response #1

One's temptation here is to try to construct a quasi-legal situation: to ask Straight to gather depositions, to stage a confrontation between Straight and Dr. Sappho, or whatever. I believe that this would be wrong, at least at this point. The whole truth and nothing but the truth is probably not discoverable here, and the search for it would only make more real the dangers of the situation. The first danger, of course, lies in students' talking about having their parents write to the college president. Mike and his friends must be made to see that the integrity of the classroom, the integrity of the enterprise in which he and Dr. Sappho are mutually engaged, cannot survive violation by persons outside the enterprise. This means a promise by the chairman to talk to Dr. Sappho (to assure Mike that somebody is listening), but it also means trying to make Mike take pride in his role as a student. I would, then, promise Mike to discuss matters with Sappho, while giving most of my energies to trying to broaden his definition of his own responsibilities as a student. I would also ask him to invite all other troubled students to see me.

The next step is, of course, talking to Dr. Sappho. Here again, "truth" is not the issue. I would not seek from her a defense against the allegations but rather attempt to open a discussion about the role of one's opinions in the classroom. I would hope my line would be, "Students are reacting in these ways—let's talk about tactics." After all, it is her skills as a teacher, not her opinions, that are at issue.

These would be my procedures at this stage. Should the situation heat up, other responses might be required. I would hope that at no point, however, would the chairman lose sight of his primary function: facilitating the development of his colleagues and their students. (Charles W. Crupi, Department of English, Albion College, Albion, Michigan.)

Crupi directs our attention to the importance of the chairperson's providing initial support to her department and conveying to the student a broader definition of the intellectual enterprise. This is extremely important counsel—both for the morale of the faculty and for the mission of the institution. Less stress is placed on the issue of academic freedom. With this in mind, look at the next response. After all is said and done about teaching skills, the content of what is presented can still be an issue.

Response #2

Dr. Sappho won't be a problem for very long; self-destructive faculty end up the same as self-destructive insurance
salesmen.

Part of what makes a liberal arts college prestigious is its
tolerance for organisms that other institutions cannot tolerate.
These institutions—law, business and commerce, medicine
—spit out the idiosyncratic as quickly, as efficiently, and as
surely as Athens did four centuries before Christ. The world of
academia, thus, has a reputation to maintain. It must, in the interest of truth, find room for the Dr. Sapphos of the world.
Once that is said, I should advise Calvina Short to speak with
Dr. Sappho, maybe over coffee, and point out to her that she is
likely to catch more flies with honey than with vinegar. That is,
to the extent that her feminist views can appropriately be used
as part of the matter of her political science courses—and I
think they can be so used—she should be encouraged to
express them. She should remember that such views do not
constitute all of political science, however, and that their acceptance might be more easily achieved if she were able to be
less aggressive and offensive than she appears now to be.
Equality with men, after all, should not be considered the same
as a mandate to be as bad as the worst. (John H. Irsfeld,
Department of English, University of Nevada/Las Vegas.)

B. "Unwelcome Publicity"— Conflict Between Departments

The second case in this chapter presents an instance of conflict
between two department chairpersons—conflict stemming
from the behavior of one individual who seems determined to
promote his cause regardless of the expense to other individuals, to his department, or to his institution.

UNWELCOME PUBLICITY

All of the details of the outburst were still churning in his
mind as Jim rode his bicycle to campus Monday. The confron-

tation had occurred Friday evening at the annual faculty party.
A regular event for the past eight years, the party was a social
highpoint, and everyone looked forward to it eagerly as the
Christmas holidays drew near. Celebrating the end of the first
semester as much as the holiday season, the party was always
a lively event, with liquor flowing freely until late in the evening.

This time, however, events had been less jovial. Norm
Bond, chair of the chemistry department, really unloaded on
Jim. It was quite a scene, with loud and harsh words. The
room quickly hushed and the ugly language was heard by all.
Norm was usually a very quiet person, so his ridiculing of Jim
for poor department leadership was all the more conspicuous.
At the heart of the confrontation was Ignatius, a member of
the history department, which Jim chaired.

Ignatius Rally was an associate professor of history who
favored causes. He seemed not to have grown beyond his
anti-Vietnam days, for he appeared fulfilled only when in the
thick of some protest activity. A Marxist of sorts, he was mas-
ter of rhetoric that was inflamatory to conservative-business
ears. Worker exploitation, collusion in pricing, obscene profits, environmental rape—all the code words resided perma-
nently at the tip of his tongue, ready for use. A certain percentage of the students always found him attractive, and he
seemed to revel in their attention.

Everyone on campus knew about Ignatius. While irritat-
ing, he had previously been rather harmless. Now, however,
he had really stirred up a hornet's nest. Increasingly critical of
one of the major area industries for its failure to comply with
the spirit of environmental restraint, Rally had been featured
several times recently in the local media. The last time it had
been as leader of a student march on the company head-
quarters, with the whole group wearing gas masks and carrying a coffin to protest the early deaths that they alleged the
company's pollutants were causing.

As Norm Bond had observed, the company was the same
one that the chemistry department had been assiduously
courting for several years now in an effort to secure new laboratory equipment. Bond became furious when he saw the
march on TV. "What kind of a hare-brained outfit are you
chairing? What about displaying some maturity in the depart-

ment?" he thundered. And just what, he demanded to know, was Jim going to do to rein in Ignatius?

Yes, thought Jim as he pedaled up the hill, just what was he going to do? Ignatius was a tiresome fellow, given to self-righteousness and black-and-white analyses where others saw only ambiguity and gray. He should never have been given tenure, for he had no judgment at all. But that decision had been made long before Jim became chair the previous May. He knew that whatever he said, Ignatius was going to cite academic freedom and the First Amendment. At least that had happened in September, when Jim inquired about Ignatius' organizing of RAG (Revolutionary Attack Group), the militant student group.

So far, the institution's president had said nothing, but Jim was not sure how long he would remain silent. This kind of behavior was hurting the institution as a whole as well as the chemistry department. Jim wanted very much to provide appropriate leadership. What should he do?

One can easily imagine Ignatius claiming academic freedom in defense of his behavior. Is this persuasive? An interesting feature of this case is that the behavior occurs out of the classroom and off campus. Is that fact significant for the response of the chairperson? Other questions include the following: How should Jim approach Ignatius? What tactics should one use with a publicity-prone individual given to grandstanding? How, if at all, can Ignatius' activities and disposition be harnessed for the good of the department? What contacts, if any, should Jim initiate with the dean or president? What should Jim say to Bond?

Consider the following responses.

Response #1

Unless a considerable body of evidence indicates either that Ignatius Rally has turned his classroom into a forum on political activism or that the time he spends in pursuit of political activities has been so outrageously excessive as to make him demonstrably incompetent both as a teacher and as a scholar, then Jim neither should (ethically) nor can (legally) take any official action as department chair to constrain him. If Jim is foolish enough to press the issue—to the extent, for instance, of threatening to terminate Ignatius for cause—then both he and the institution for which he is agent would be actionable. The president of the institution, who so far has "said nothing," has exercised better judgment in this situation than what Jim is contemplating. At least insofar as his official behavior is concerned, Jim should emulate his president. It is perhaps trite to point out that, while Ignatius may lack maturity and judgment and while his ideas and actions may be objectionable to some (or even to everybody!), he nonetheless possesses fundamental rights of free expression, which he must be allowed to exercise without fear of reprisal.

This is not to say that there is not a problem in human relations here that calls for some kind of prompt action. It is unlikely that the chemical company's decision whether or not to provide new equipment for Norm Bond's laboratory is going to be materially influenced by the behavior of an outspoken associate professor in the history department. What is important is that Norm thinks it is, and, let's face it, he may be right. Angry at the prospect of seeing several years' work go for nought, he has been driven to an uncharacteristic public display of temper. Let us be charitable and suggest, also, that under the influence of the annual faculty party he has forgotten, but of course only temporarily, the fundamental principles and freedoms upon which places of higher learning must be based. In any case, he has publicly insulted the chairman of the history department, demeaned one of its members, and embarrassed himself. As Jim cycles pensively to class this Monday morning, Norm Bond is very likely somewhere feeling remorseful and foolish, wishing there were only some way he could gracefully recant. Jim can and should provide such an opportunity lest Bond's embarrassment deteriorate into an entrenched, defensive animosity toward Jim *and* his department. This is the stuff of which enduring department feuds are made—it is up to someone to ensure that this does not happen.

Jim, then, should arrange somehow to meet with Norm informally. It is tempting to suggest that in the interests of broadening perspectives he might include Ignatius in this session, but, from what we know of Ignatius, this is likely to lead to more conflict rather than to reconciliation. No, let Jim and Norm meet together to lament the apparently insoluble problems and disappointments of department leadership. If Jim is subtly persuasive, Norm should leave such a meeting informed by a better understanding of the proper ethical and legal boundaries of a chairman's authority. Jim should leave with a sense that he has defused what is potentially a very harmful situation and regained a colleague's goodwill. This is apparently a small institution (if the entire faculty attends one party), and since the principals in this dispute have resolved their differences, that will soon become known and the matter will quickly be forgotten. (John Feaster, Associate Dean, College of Arts and Sciences, Valparaiso University, Valparaiso, Indiana.)

Response #2

Why should Jim do anything? My initial advice to Jim would be to keep pedaling his Schwinn until his unwarranted embarrassment from the episode has worn off. But this response might well lead to Jim's being identified within his department and the campus community as a weak chairman who can be intimidated by other chairmen or the central administration. Clearly he must climb down from his bicycle seat and assume some sort of position.

Professor Ignatius Rally indeed might be a tiresome boor given to self-righteousness and possessing little judgment. But what about the judgment of Norm Bond, the chemistry department chairman? Can he really believe that it is within Jim's authority as department chairman to police the political behavior of his faculty members? What could have possessed him to use the annual faculty Christmas party as the forum for his attack on another department chairman? Who is being boorish and self-righteous?

In response, Jim should do two things. First, he should invite Bond to his office for a professional discussion of his position: Why he believes Ignatius is within his rights as a private citizen to protest the company's polluting activities, why his authority as chairman does not extend to sanctions of the lawful political behavior of his faculty members, why he feels Bond's attack was inappropriately delivered in an inappropriate forum. Bond should be given every opportunity to apologize publicly for this outburst, and a note on the meeting should be sent to Jim's dean.

Second, Jim should hold a similar session with Rally, recounting the incident at the party and outlining his position on Rally's behavior. Jim should make it clear that he is neither condoning or sanctioning Rally's political activities—while pointing out that other members of the academic community might try to use the threat of the loss of a few Bunsen burners as justification for penalizing him. Rally should be reminded of the distinction between his constitutional rights as a private person and his official position as a faculty member, and be cautioned that others might possibly confuse the two. A note on this meeting should be entered in Rally's file, to be retained within the department.

Finally, Jim should remind himself of the long-standing tradition of free speech and free thought in the institution's community. Should his institution show signs of violating this tradition in catering to the interests of the local industrial community, he should wipe the pollution off his résumé and circulate it in cleaner environments. (Walter J. Jaehnig, Head, Journalism and Telecommunication, University of Wyoming, Laramie, Wyoming.)

Conflict between departments can also stem from disagreements on the staffing of interdisciplinary courses as well as on shared endeavors or needs, such as courses in statistics. Joint appointments and degree programs jointly administered can also present challenges.

C. "Mary Workhard"—Conflict Between Younger and Older Faculty

Chairpersons can experience other forms of conflict within the department. "Mary Workhard" illustrates the cleavage between younger and older faculty members that occasionally occurs—particularly at institutions that have attempted to upgrade themselves in recent years. The older faculty members at such institutions often feel that the "rules of the game" have been changed on them and that their contributions over the years are not appreciated. They contend that they have invested their energies in the institution rather than their own careers. Now, when their energies are reduced or depleted, the institution is rewarding quite different activities. The younger faculty members, in contrast, feel that higher demands are unfairly placed upon them and that the older members are not pulling their share. Severe morale problems can develop as a result.

MARY WORKHARD

Chairperson Mary Workhard once thought she was making some progress with the department. However, yesterday's unanimous vote of the tenured department members against Sam Sharp had now shown that notion to be a conceit. Having just learned of the outcome, she left the office with a splitting headache.

Her own academic credentials were quite adequate, she knew, but not what one would call distinguished. Nonetheless, she had worked hard to get them, supporting two children all the while. Nor had she stopped striving when she finished her terminal degree. Part of one's responsibility as a professional, she felt, was to continue the journey of inquiry that only begins upon completing the terminal degree. She believed this ought to be a way of life for all teachers.

Mary did not feel that one had to publish lengthy treatises

to merit tenure. Certainly she had not done so herself. She did feel, however, that one ought to make a consistent effort to stay abreast with what others in the field were doing and saying. And there ought to be some evidence of that effort; publications would indeed be one sign, but so would informal presentations to department colleagues and student majors.

Senior colleagues in the department, however, evidently had a different view. They had just voted to deny tenure to an individual who had been exemplary in such respects. During his six years at the institution, Sam Sharp had made major contributions in both teaching and research. He had been generous with his time in advising students and imaginative in his suggestions about curricular innovations. Mary knew that some students were alienated by his high standards, for he made considerable demands on his classes. And his personality was not the most pleasing, as he could be quite abrasive when in pursuit of an idea. But there was no question in her mind that he was precisely the sort of instructor that the undergraduate college needed.

At her interview for the job the previous spring, the college dean and president had both indicated that the department was particularly weak and that they were looking to the new chairperson for leadership. Upon inquiring, she was told that institutional policy prohibited awarding tenure to anyone without at least a year's experience at the institution, but that she should have no trouble. The important thing was to generate some excitement among the department members.

Seven of the other ten department members were tenured. In Mary's judgment, the other two probationary members were also very promising individuals, products of the new, hungrier class of academics and determined to use their talents to their best advantage. They knew the gypsylike existence that awaited them if released from the institution and therefore were working hard to be good teachers, scholars, and advisors.

The seven older, tenured members were middle-aged carry-overs from the time the institution was a teachers college. Three of them did not have the terminal degree. None of them had published. When Mary talked with them individually about Sam Sharp's tenure situation a few weeks before, she got the strong impression that they would oppose him.

No one said so outright, but she sensed that they resented his accomplishments. When she pressed them for comments, most alluded to his ambition and excessive aggressiveness. Two of them also pointed out that the college was a teaching institution and that anyone who found time for scholarship must be neglecting the classroom.

Mary knew that for her to recommend tenure for Sharp would almost surely be perceived by the tenured faculty of the department as a rejection of them. Such a reaction could result in a bad setback to her efforts to involve them again in the excitement of inquiry. On the other hand, to support a tenure denial would be a terrible violation of her academic conscience and a disservice to Sam Sharp. Either way, she knew she could count on some student opposition.

How should she proceed and what strategies should she adopt?

This case illustrates some of the challenges facing the department chairperson who comes into the position from outside the institution. How is he or she to mitigate the conflict and reinvigorate the department when faced with suspicion from the older faculty members? How can the chairperson's newness be used to advantage? What strengths in the department might be built upon?

Additionally, this case suggests some of the pressure that a new, untenured chairperson can feel. Should Mary have sought more concrete assurance from the administration that her efforts to reinvigorate the department would not adversely affect her tenure prospects? What risks might that have involved? The two responses that follow provide very different answers to some of these questions.

Response #1

Mary has been put into a position that is as difficult to resolve as any that I have encountered. She is an untenured chairperson brought in from outside the university by the administration to make changes in the direction of academic quality and professional involvement in a heavily tenured department. Clearly she must have either the majority of the faculty behind her or the security of tenure before she can proceed. The support of the dean and president alone is not enough.

Since Mary needs this job for economic reasons and has presumably not done the publishing necessary to find a suitable alternative, I believe she should carefully reflect on the department's opinions during her probationary year. With the assumption that the department's tenure recommendations are normally followed by those who grant tenure, she cannot risk opposing them at this early stage in her chairmanship. She should point out to the faculty members individually that, while Sam has certain attributes she feels are definite assets to the department, she will pass along their recommendation. The chances are excellent that there are other Sam Sharps hunting for jobs in academia, with personalities less abrasive to the department. Regretfully, this particular one should be written off. He is the victim of a stagnant department. Mary needs to be very careful that she does not turn out to be one as well.

Mary's major task, aside from obtaining tenure for herself, is to spark up the deadwood faculty members so that they will not feel threatened by the next high-achieving and lively untenured professor to be voted on. She needs to change the department perspective that she is to represent. The time is ripe for faculty development. Depending on the institution's and the individuals' circumstances, this might involve such changes as a job transfer to the alumni office for an old-timer, a new course assignment team-taught with a younger, untenured professor, small grants for course innovations, or the specific mentorship of one new instructor. In any case, Mary needs to spend a great deal of time encouraging and motivating the individuals in her department to develop some pride in their own, and thus the department's, productivity. With this strategy, the department tenure committee has a better chance to be more objective about and more receptive to the retention of another competent, but more congenial, untenured professor. (Elizabeth V. Swenson, Associate Professor and Chairperson, Department of Psychology, John Carroll University, Cleveland, Ohio.)

The personal fortunes of the chairperson loom large in Swenson's analysis. Mary's effectiveness is seen as a function of her own untenured status, and the fortunes of the department outweigh those of Sam. For a quite different perspective, consider the following analysis. Although they differ in their counsel about Sam, both responses contain good suggestions about ways to reinvigorate the older, tenured faculty.

Response #2

Mary Workhard has an excellent opportunity to establish herself as a strong, conscientious, competent chairperson, to determine the direction in which the department will move, and to bring needed new perspectives to her tenured faculty by obeying her "academic conscience" and recommending tenure for Sam Sharp. To retreat or to compromise in this instance will assign the department for an indefinite period of time to a status of mediocrity and will diminish her role, her authority, and her reputation as chairperson. True, the seven tenured members of the department may feel "threatened" temporarily by Sharp and, in fact, may be jealous of him and his achievement, or even annoyed at what they perceive as his "ambition" and "excessive aggressiveness." It is possible, however, that as individuals they may secretly respect him for his zest and his initiative.

At any rate, Mary has the opportunity to demonstrate the need to upgrade the department and to encourage those who are innovative, constructive, and progressive in their approaches to teaching. She also is faced with the challenge of convincing the seven tenured members of their continuing value and their responsibilities to the department. She can stress in a number of ways her recognition of the fact that teachers colleges generally do not subscribe to the dictum "Publish or perish" for faculty tenure, but that they do have a variety of other ways to judge effective teaching and to formulate criteria for promotion and tenure. Among important activities are participation in college life, staff-conducted studies involving curriculum, construction of tests and measurements of student performance, new courses of study leading to such things as understanding of the place of man in society, studies in comparison of teaching and teacher training, etc. In short, by advocating a combination of the best of the old and the best of the new, Mary can bring new vigor and an improved image to the department over which she presides.

As chairperson, Mary Workhard also must assess realistically the changing attitudes and moods of students. Though some of Sharp's students may express dissatisfaction because of his high standards and his demands, they will probably develop and show greater respect for him if the standards of the entire department are raised. The other two probationary faculty members, who seem "promising individuals, products of the new, hungrier class of academics ... determined to use their talent to the best advantage," will be heartened by Sam Sharp's retention and tenure. Indeed, the entire college community, department, teachers and students should benefit. (Estelle W. Taylor, Chairman, Department of English, Howard University, Washington, D.C.)

D. "The Frustrated Peacemaker"— The Polarized Department

The chairperson in the following case study is feeling different pressures. The conflict in his department is between faculty of different subdisciplines, not of different tenure status. The division is aggravated by the keen competition between two very powerful personalities. Polarized, the department is in serious danger of crushing students and junior faculty who get caught in the middle or who happen to be aligned with the wrong side at some crucial moment.

THE FRUSTRATED PEACEMAKER

Joe remembered from his own graduate days at Yale how certain faculty members could never seem to get to the joint meetings that the students arranged with colleagues at Harvard. The rumor was that the Yale faculty would find out ahead of time whether faculty from Harvard would be at the meeting, or vice versa, and either decline to attend or accept accordingly. There seemed to be some kind of territorial sense involved. It was as though one possessed certain areas of inquiry, and challenges were not welcome.

The Yale memories were old but amazingly relevant to his current situation. As chair of the psychology department at State University, he had to deal regularly with inflated egos and status-consciousness. He felt sufficiently confident of his own credentials not to be intimidated by any of this, but the faculty could certainly be difficult. Two professors in particular were quite divisive forces within the department.

Ideologically, the two had little in common. In fact, they represented positions of extreme opposition on most curricular issues. One was a clinical psychologist, the other an experimental psychologist. At a larger institution they would probably be in different departments. Here they had intellectual contempt for each other, and their personalities were not very accommodating. Each viewed power as a zero-sum commodity: if one gained, then the other lost. In principle it was fine to have two such luminaries in one department, but in practice it was nothing but a headache.

In principle it was fine, because each should spur the other to even greater accomplishments. In the absence of competition, Joe believed, people tended to slide, to regress toward the average. But those two were so competitive that they seemed to polarize the department. Other faculty members and many of the students seemed to be in either one camp or the other. As a result, apparently innocent issues were regularly blown up to near-cosmic dimensions. Nothing could be discussed without being interpreted to the advantage of one or the other. Everything was personalized.

Joe had been named chairperson by the dean the previous year in a peacemaking effort of the administration. Although the old chairperson had retired, budget problems forced the department to give up a slot. Otherwise the dean would have recruited the new chairperson from outside. Joe knew that he had been selected because he was the only one not identified with either side. The dean had been frank, indicating that she was looking to him for leadership and recommendations on reducing the turmoil within the department.

Joe had noticed that the alignment of department faculty on different issues seemed fairly stable—breaking down regularly into the two camps. Things had come to a head again recently, when the department promotion and tenure committee failed to agree in their report on Carla Head, a talented and well-published clinical psychologist. "Inadequate statistical skills," the experimentalists claimed. The committee vote reflected the department division, for it was evenly split. In his own report Joe recommended tenure for Dr. Head and explained for the benefit of upper-level administrators the animosities within the department.

Joe knew that the department was ripe for a grievance. If Head were denied tenure, he felt sure that she would file—charging arbitrary and capricious, as well as discriminatory, behavior. Students, too, could explode at any moment, the clinically oriented claiming harsh treatment at the hands of the experimentalists, and vice versa. Joe felt as if he was sitting on a powder keg.

Preparing to meet with the dean to review the case of Dr. Head and other matters within the department, Joe pondered what general recommendations he could provide her. Formally dividing the department into two was one possibility he had considered. He felt reluctant to recommend this to the dean, however, for it would be frank admission of failure. It was a shame within the academic community, of all places, to yield to such unfortunate fragmentation. There ought to be a way to heal the division and to unite the functions.

Do you have any suggestions for Joe? What are some steps that the chairperson should explore in order to reduce tension and redirect the department?

Consider the following two responses.

Response #1

This case study is extremely well described. In fact, it is described so well that I found myself feeling thankful that I am not in Joe's position. At the extreme, problems of this kind are often not solvable—short of a real brouhaha.

In spite of all the problems, splitting the department should not yet be considered. Such a split would really damage the graduate program, not to mention the department's reputation, and there is no indication that a majority of the faculty would favor such a move.

However, there is virtually no chance that the two professors will ever be cooperative colleagues. The only glimmer of hope lies in the fact that Joe is not identified with either camp. I would encourage him to build a larger group of neutrals, a move I believe he could do slowly, over a period of years. If successful, he could reach a point where there are really only two adversaries isolated from everyone else. To do this, however, Joe needs to be clearly perceived as a fair chairperson who is working for the best interests of the department. It takes a lot of energy to maintain a feud, and I am guessing that there must be others who are tired of all the nonsense. At best, however, it will still take years.

There is also one other possibility. The case study does not specify that the merit of the two professors is high and equal in both cases, and my comments above are based on the assumption that they are both highly and equally meritorious. If this is incorrect and there are differences in their research and teaching contributions, then Joe has another option: to put the squeeze on the weaker contributor. This is, of course, unpleasant and difficult, but the best interests of the department leave Joe little choice. (David G. McDonald, Associate Dean, College of Arts and Sciences, University of Missouri/Columbia.)

Response #2

The heart of this problem is clearly the highly competitive relationship between the two professors and their apparent

unwillingness or inability to accept or accommodate the personalities or ideologies of the other. It seems obvious that they
neither like nor want to like each other. It also appears that
each has been allowed to "do his thing", to revel in his power
to wield influence over a segment of the department and of the
student body.

The two professors are effectively "running" the department: everyone else (the dean, former and present department
chairpersons, teachers, and students) is reacting to them, as
well as to each issue, curricular or otherwise, that results from
their relationship. The Carla Head issue is a messy one and
will certainly have to be dealt with soon, as will many other
problems in the future. The basic situation, however, will continue until the root of the problem, the two professors themselves, is confronted and changed. Strong, decisive department leadership is called for here, leadership that apparently
has been lacking.

The scenario does not indicate whether attempts to challenge and confront them have been attempted. I will assume
that even if some efforts have been made in the past, they must
be resumed and done so immediately and forcefully.

I suggest that Joe and the dean get their heads together and
decide how they should proceed. It is important that three
ideas be communicated to the men:

1. Each professor must be made to understand and acknowledge that despite the many good things he has undoubtedly been doing, he is a source of disunity and
   tension in the department.

2. Each should be given an incentive to change; for the
   good of the department and of all concerned, each is
   being asked to sacrifice some of his personal preferences
   by being more flexible and open to the other person and
   his ideas.

3. Each should also know that if he does not evidence some
   effort to cooperate, punitive action will be taken (for ex-

ample, loss of salary increment, or something else that
would be important to each).

If several serious attempts to effect behavior modification
have failed, stronger measures should be enforced, possibly a
dismissal case. This certainly would be a last resort.

I would recommend that after Joe and the dean have
decided on their plan of action (with each step clearly worked
out), the two of them together meet first with one of the teachers, then with the other one, then with both together. There
may well be a need for several subsequent meetings to assess
progress in the interaction between the two. Other processes
may also be tried if deemed beneficial.

The first compromise should be on the part of the experimentalist in regard to Carla Head's tenure. If the dean supports
the department chairperson's recommendation, then the experimentalist should be asked to reconsider and support the
administrators' position. If he doesn't cooperate, tenure
should be granted anyway, and the experimentalist should be
confronted head on. The tenure decision is a critical one in the
eventual reconciliation process. It must be handled with great
sensitivity, yet decisively.

There will always be irreconcilable problems, divisiveness,
and tension in this department as long as the two psycholog-
ists are allowed to continue behaving as they have behaved
and unless they are confronted with the situation and challenged to make efforts toward some degree of reconciliation
and compromise. A strong and forceful department head with
strong and forceful support from the dean is needed in this situation. (Brother Vincent Malham, Chairperson, Christian
Brothers College, Memphis, Tennessee.)

E. "The Ph.D. Candidate"—Dealing with Favorites

A variation on the polarized department presented above
occurs when the division falls according to age rather than

tenure status, subdiscipline, or personality. Individual faculty members can have their favorites among students, and such preferences can create serious problems, as the following case study shows.

THE Ph.D. CANDIDATE

As chairperson, Sylvia found herself right in the middle of the department fracas over Mrs. Hilda Cartworth. Hilda was a nice, middle-aged Ph.D. student in the English department. Well-connected through her marriage to one of the prominent community leaders, Hilda had been encouraged several years earlier to pursue the doctorate by various senior English-department members who were social intimates. Given her clear interest in literature and her insightful comments on a wide range of novelists and poets, they convinced her over one dinner or another that she should have no difficulty in completing the degree.

Thus stimulated and encouraged, Hilda applied and was admitted. Sylvia had not been involved in any of the admissions decisions that year but, looking back, she felt that Hilda's friends on the committee must have been persuasive. Certainly Hilda's subsequent record in the department did not suggest any abundance of talent. Her coursework had not been distinguished. She had passed her comprehensive examination only on the second time and even that had been barely acceptable. The problem now was her inability to complete the dissertation. She was on her fourth draft of the first two chapters and each revision seemed only to secure her more deeply in difficulty.

The junior faculty was all for dropping her from the rolls and had strongly pressed their case to Sylvia. The problem was that the senior faculty was exerting equal pressure in behalf of Hilda. In fact, they had dropped several strong suggestions that the junior faculty simply resented Hilda's friendships. In order to observe every appearance of propriety, few of the senior faculty had taught her courses, and none had sat on her comprehensive exams committee or read any of the dissertation material. Having observed such scrupulous measures, the senior faculty was now simply outraged that others in the department were prepared to take advantage of the situation and cashier Cartworth. So they told Sylvia, hinting darkly at how they might have to retaliate if this vendetta against Cartworth were to continue.

To complicate matters, Hilda had herself recently indicated to Sylvia that she was prepared to take matters to the president or even to the courts, charging sexual and age bias if she was dropped.

How should Sylvia sort through this issue and resolve it?

The proper role of the chair in this case is by no means obvious. Drawbacks, if not dangers, seem associated with the various alternatives. Consider the following two differing responses.

Response #1

Sylvia is clearly caught in the middle in the case of Hilda Cartworth's attempt to earn a Ph.D. in English. She must attempt to balance the views of the two disparate faculty groups while concerning herself with a potential discrimination charge by Mrs. Cartworth.

The first step Sylvia must take is to determine the legitimacy of the claims and counterclaims concerning Mrs. Cartworth's ability to successfully complete and defend a doctoral dissertation. Without firsthand knowledge gained through examination of Mrs. Cartworth's work, she is at a disadvantage in assessing these claims. Thus she must examine Mrs. Cartworth's efforts on the dissertation to date.

Having reached a conclusion concerning Mrs. Cartworth's ability, Sylvia's next step should be to assume the role of an informed mediator in dealing with the senior and junior faculty. As a mediator, she must bring both sides together with a common basis for discussion. At present no such basis exists, because the senior faculty has not read either Mrs. Cartworth's exams or drafts of her dissertation. Until they do so, there is no rational basis for discussion. Thus, Sylvia must prevail upon some of the more responsible senior faculty to evaluate Mrs. Cartworth's work, preferably one or more individuals who are not quite as close to Mrs. Cartworth on a social basis.

Once a common base of knowledge is established, Sylvia can begin her role as a mediator; she cannot be an impartial one, because she needs to guide any discussions to a decision reflecting her own professional judgments. If attempts at mediation fail, Sylvia must assume the role of an arbitrator and support what she believes to be the correct view. To allow the present state of events to continue would be highly disruptive for the department, perhaps leading to a permanent breach between senior and junior faculty.

If, through mediation, the department reaches the conclusion that Mrs. Cartworth should be dropped from the Ph.D. program, Sylvia should enlist the aid of one or more of the senior faculty in breaking the news to Mrs. Cartworth. Such a move would assure her that she is not a victim of discrimination.

In the event the decision to drop Mrs. Cartworth from the program is reached via the arbitration route, Sylvia must deliver the news herself and convince both Mrs. Cartworth and the senior faculty that no discrimination is involved. Failure to convince Mrs. Cartworth could lead to the filing of a discrimination complaint. Failure to convince the faculty could lead to the complaint being sustained. As long as a student is dropped from a program for purely academic reasons a discrimination complaint will not be sustained, but even a hint of discrimination could give life to such a claim.

Successful mediation may produce a favorable decision for Mrs. Cartworth, as may arbitration. If this proves to be the case, Sylvia should use her power to appoint a different dissertation committee for Mrs. Cartworth—one that is not unduly critical of her because of her contacts with the senior faculty, but not closely identified with her. (Michael C. Walker, Head, Finance, Insurance, Real Estate and Law, North Texas State University, Denton, Texas.)

Response #2

This case has several considerations that seem highly relevant and important but that in reality are not. Foremost among these are the facts that (1) Cartworth is a nontraditional student, (2) her husband is locally prominent, and (3) she has threatened to take her complaints to the president or to the courts. These facts should cause Sylvia to do her homework thoroughly, choose her words carefully, keep the dean informed, and so on, but they should have no bearing on Cartworth's candidacy in the department.

Unfortunately, the problem has complicated roots. It would appear that the senior faculty had a lapse in professional judgment, the junior faculty complicated the error, and Sylvia was remiss in not having dealt with the problem years earlier. At the very least, Sylvia should (through the appropriate faculty committee, etc.) initiate a review of department procedures in general, with an eye toward preventing this problem in the future.

With regard to Cartworth in particular, the only question is whether or not there is a faculty member who will agree to serve as the dissertation supervisor. Quite frankly, I feel that the department has a strong moral obligation to ensure that there is one, but the department chair does not have the authority to force anyone to do it. The status of a graduate student is a matter to be decided by the mentor and the student's committee, not the department chair.

On the other hand, Sylvia does have the option of proposing deadlines for faculty adoption. For example, her department could adopt a policy that students must complete their Ph.D. requirements in X years, a policy that all departments should have anyway. Beyond that, Sylvia should simply let nature take its course. (David G. McDonald, Associate Dean, College of Arts and Sciences, University of Missouri/Columbia.)

Potentially destructive conflict seems to be an inevitable

part of human affairs. No chairperson will be able to escape having to deal with at least some form of it. The individual who shrinks from all forms of confrontation is therefore not likely to enjoy the position or be successful in it. On the other hand, the person who is excessively combative will probably keep the waters too roiled, and his or her department will suffer as a result. The trick, of course, is finding that middle path and staying on it.

CHAPTER FOUR

Performance Counseling

PERFORMANCE COUNSELING and dealing with unsatisfactory performance are major concerns of department chairpersons. The ambiguity of the position of chair is underscored in these activities, as it is in the prior processes of evaluation, which may lead to awareness of the need for counseling. Such efforts tend to separate the chair from faculty colleagues and to challenge the concept of collegiality. For both reasons, many chairs regard performance counseling as onerous.

Of course, problems of unsatisfactory performance may not materialize; but being aware that they might occur is in itself a step toward preventing them. Awareness of present or developing problems usually calls for some form of intervention or counseling. It is natural to delay this counseling in the hope that the problems will correct themselves. Occasionally this does happen. Far more frequently, however, things simply get worse—sometimes slowly and gradually, and sometimes with surprising abruptness.

In any case, counseling should be regarded as a two-way situation. It is not merely an occasion for the chairperson to

73

communicate his or her concerns to the department member. Of course, any such communication should include ample positive comments about the individual's accomplishments and contributions. In fact, concern about problems should be conveyed only in the context of appreciation for successes.

In addition, however, such a session provides an opportunity for the chairperson to be given further insight into specific department activities and personalities. It also gives the faculty member a chance to suggest various improvements or alternatives regarding the problems at hand. Unless matters have deteriorated to the point that termination is the only course of action, performance counseling should always emphasize improvement and development—of both the individual and the department.

Some instances of unsatisfactory performance flow from a mismatch of faculty member and assignment. For example, someone whose main gifts lie in teaching graduate students may be struggling with three classes of lower-division undergraduates. The reverse can also occur. These situations may have developed because of curricular and scheduling necessities, or they may represent the individual's determination to try something new or to move into more prestigious areas. As a result, different counseling situations and strategies are in order.

Other instances of unsatisfactory performance are more clearly rooted in the individual, in his or her character or personal circumstances. The alcoholic professor, for instance, is all too common and can present an especially agonizing challenge. Only he or she can really correct the underlying problem. The chairperson can but outline clearly the areas of unsatisfactory performance, establish a firm timetable for the necessary improvements, and stick to it.

The performance of the faculty member with a protracted illness at home or other disruptions in his or her family life can be expected to fall off. Certainly those who are undergoing the trauma of divorce can display erratic behavior. Special departmental arrangements may need to be made to help the individual through such difficult periods. Those with special physical or emotional disabilities may require long-term solutions, and the college dean or other administrators should be consulted.

Of special concern for chairpersons should be the junior faculty. Those with probationary status need careful counseling to understand clearly the institution's and department's requirements for tenure. Of course, opportunities must be presented for these requirements to be met. Careful monitoring is then in order to nip in the bud any unsatisfactory performance.

Nor should those who are not on a tenure track be neglected. Assistance in learning of and securing other positions should be provided. The chairperson and other members of the department need also to be sensitive to ways in which the skills and hence the marketability of such individuals can be advanced. Certainly the department has some obligation to help, and not just to use, these people.

Chairpersons may also need to be alert for special opportunities and challenges for faculty in their middle years as the excitement that accompanied earlier, fresh experience fades and as the tedium of repetition increases. We know more now about various patterns and cycles of change in the development of the typical adult. In some situations chairpersons may need to make special efforts to present career changes in a favorable and viable light, and then to support faculty in pursuing them.

The case studies in this chapter illustrate a few of the recurring challenges that chairpersons face in performance counseling and dealing with unsatisfactory performance. Special emphasis is placed upon various teaching inadequacies, abuses of student assistants, and unproductive or deadwood faculty. Other problems could also have been presented.

A. "Baby Sociology"—A Teaching Problem in the Multisection Course

"Baby Sociology" features a senior professor who has become a major teaching problem. His students are unenthusiastic about his class, and he seems to share their lack of enthusiasm. But he, not the course content, is the problem. The situation is complicated by department policy earlier adopted more under duress than with enthusiasm. In addition, the chairperson has the psychological burden of being only an associate professor. Nevertheless, the professor must be dealt with.

BABY SOCIOLOGY

It had been another long, stressful day, and Max Parsons was looking forward to a drink with Lois Whyte, his predecessor as chairperson of the sociology department. He hoped to get her views on a couple of perplexing issues. At the heart of his current problems was the basic introductory course, Sociology 101.

Baby Soc, as it was known among the faculty, was a real student-credit-hour generator for the department. The department had been able to secure it as a basic option in the distribution requirements when the undergraduate curriculum was revamped three years ago. The course immediately attracted large numbers of students. In fact, Dr. Whyte had to set up six sections in order to handle the demand.

At that time the university senate had stipulated that regular faculty members, not merely teaching fellows, were to be the main staff for courses meeting the distribution requirements. Graduate students could be used as graders and discussion-section assistants, but the courses had to be taught by full-time faculty. There had even been a recommendation that senior-level faculty should be involved. Although it had not been stated as a requirement, it was well known that both the arts and sciences dean and the university vice-president for academic affairs strongly supported the idea.

Dr. Whyte had also felt strongly that the senior faculty should be involved in the basic introductory sociology course. She had reasoned that their teaching skills could only be improved by this. Also, they would be able to draw upon a much broader range of knowledge than could the younger faculty. In addition, she thought, exposure to the top guns should enhance the attractiveness of the department among uncommitted students.

At any rate, she pushed through the department policy that all of the tenured professors had to teach at least one of the sections each year. Parsons had just recently joined the faculty at the time this was occurring. It had seemed clear to him then that few of the tenured professors were really enthusiastic about the prospect of teaching the introductory course. Whyte had appealed to the dictates of professionalism, though, and the policy passed without a negative note.

An associate professor, Parsons had been chairperson of the department for two years now. His biggest problem was staffing and coordinating the introductory course. Just today, for instance, five students had come to see him requesting a transfer from one section to another. Dr. Thick, they claimed, was just not a very good instructor. He seemed to resent having to teach the course, for he was frequently late to class and more often than not made derogatory comments about their level of academic preparation.

Parsons was not surprised by their report, for he had heard similar complaints from other students. Thick was not the only problem instructor: of the eight sections, two others were also suffering from an exodus of students. Thick's class was the most troublesome, however, and if the five students were to leave, his section would be below the minimum-enrollment level.

The students had been quite insistent in wanting a transfer. Tomorrow would be the last day in the semester that such a request could be made. They finally left his office only when he promised them a response in the morning. This was one of the issues on which he wanted advice from Lois Whyte.

An additional problem was at hand with the common syllabus: it seemed to be observed mainly in the breach. In fact, a fairly frequent student complaint was that the faculty did not follow the outline. Students in the different sections who compared notes in preparation for examinations would often discover that different material had been covered and that they had little idea what the common exam was to cover.

Parsons had spoken with the faculty about the complaints the previous semester. He had emphasized the importance of honoring the common syllabus. No one had disagreed, and he hoped that there would not be a problem again this time. He wondered about the merit of a department committee that would review the introductory course. Its staffing would be a delicate matter, he knew, because senior faculty would be sensitive to criticism from junior colleagues. At any rate, he wanted to get Whyte's reaction to the idea.

He also wanted to talk to her about Dr. Thick, for he had little confidence in Thick's improvement. Parsons had spoken with Thick a week earlier about the number of students who had already requested a transfer. Thick had cited his own high standards and the diminished academic capabilities of current students. Parsons had the clear impression that Thick was not too concerned about the transfers, or at least that he was not going to acknowledge it.

Lois Whyte was already waiting at a table. How should she advise Parsons?

Some specific questions include: What should Parsons do about the students wanting to transfer? How precisely can the problems of a common syllabus be handled? How can this issue be separated from academic freedom in the presentation of material? How can the dynamics of the relationship between the junior and the senior professors be improved? What is the best way of dealing with Professor Thick? Should special exceptions in the policy be made for those senior faculty who seem unable to deal with freshmen? Consider the following responses.

Response #1

Parsons faces two problems: the immediate problem of what to tell the five students and the deeper problem of the lack of enthusiasm for Baby Soc among the tenured professors, as well as their failure to honor the common syllabus. If I were Lois Whyte, I would advise Parsons as follows:

1. Thick's attitude toward his participation in Baby Soc may be unchangeable, but his practice of coming late to class and making derogatory comments (assuming this is true, and

Parsons should check it with Thick) is professionally unaccept-
able and must stop immediately. This point is unnegotiable
and should be communicated firmly by Parsons to Thick this
evening. Parsons can assure the students that such practices
will cease.

2. The more serious problem, of course, involves Thick's
attitude toward Baby Soc, especially because this attitude is
shared by others. Whyte needs to consider seriously the possibility that the whole issue of staffing Baby Soc needs to be
reexamined. It may, after all, be true that not all of the senior
faculty need to teach the course; junior faculty (and some
willing senior faculty) may be able to handle it quite well. In
any event, this issue, as well as that of the common syllabus,
needs to be rethought constructively. Parsons should therefore
appoint a department committee of the whole to review the
course and its staffing. What is of utmost importance is that
the members of the sociology faculty feel that they can turn
their disenchantment into a workable proposal regarding the
course.

It is also important for Parsons to communicate to the arts
and sciences dean and to the university vice-president for academic affairs his decision to reexamine the course, because the
present arrangement simply does not work. (George L. Goodwin, Chair, Theology Department, The College of Saint
Catherine, St. Paul, Minnesota.)

Practicality must figure prominently in the value system of
any chairperson. The following response elaborates upon this
theme and provides further suggestions.

Response #2

The key to addressing this case is to determine whether
this is a "people problem" or a problem of policy. I must assume that before the department began to associate seniority
and experience with quality instruction there was a problem.

Since Lois Whyte already is known to support the policy of having senior faculty teach courses fulfilling the distribution requirement, I will assume that Whyte is biased toward the policy; as a good former administrator, however, she will be open to change.

If I were Whyte, I would not give specific solutions but suggest strategies for arriving at a decision. First, I would discuss how we might gather information from students and faculty to define the problem more precisely. Could we do some research on the effects of having the senior faculty teach these courses? Perhaps a questionnaire could be designed to obtain necessary information. A meeting of the faculty could be arranged to bring out feelings, experiences, and directions.

By all means, we would discuss the political realities. What does it mean to have the support of the arts and sciences dean and the university vice-president for academic affairs on this issue? Could a short-range decision have long-range unfavorable consequences for the department in efforts to obtain a higher budget or new faculty positions? Does the upper echelon have its standing closely tied to this policy in any way?

Should Whyte suggest that the students who want to transfer see Dr. Thick? What is the institution's policy in this regard? If the students do not have to have the instructor's permission to transfer, their requests should be honored. It is not likely that Parsons could have time to contact the students and the students, in turn, have time to contact Thick. Besides, if Thick's approval is not necessary, this is further evidence to use in making a case for a change in the program.

Finally, I would explore variations on the policy of having senior faculty teach the distribution courses. Such variations would be in keeping with the spirit of the policy but would be educationally more efficient. Not every senior faculty member may want to teach these courses, and maybe the courses could be handled on a voluntary basis. Could incentives be used to attract volunteers to teach the courses? Could perhaps a key professor be used as the main instructor and other senior professors be used as guest lecturers? Could the main common examination be modified in some way to allow for more flexibility?

I believe Whyte's role is to stimulate ideas, offer support, and provide realistic responses. Parsons needs to solve his own problems and should not be given solutions. Indeed, there seldom is a single best solution. The alternatives need to be weighed in relation to their feasibility and their consequences, both positive and negative. (David A. Groth, Vice-President/Educational Services, Community College of Denver, Denver, Colorado.)

Generating enthusiasm for teaching the undesirable courses, reigniting the tired teachers or researchers, handling the flood of student complaints—all of these can become the lot of the chairperson.

B. "The Course Sequence"—Challenges of Course Coordination

The radical individualist in department matters can emerge in other ways, too. Coordination between courses can be as difficult as coordination among the various sections of one course. "The Course Sequence" illustrates some of the problems that can emerge in the effort to mesh the intentions of the instructor with the requirements of the course.

THE COURSE SEQUENCE

Harry Jones was wondering why he had ever sought the position of department chairperson. One reason for his black mood had just walked out the door. Roger Grimm was a tenured associate professor of history responsible for a key course in the development of American economic institutions. The course was the second in a series of three, and it was important that the objectives in the syllabus be fully met. Otherwise students would be unprepared for the final course and the integrity of whole sequence was threatened.

That was, in fact, precisely what was happening, for Grimm was failing to meet these goals. Several students had come by to complain to Jones about the course. Invariably, it seemed, Grimm would get bogged down along the way and the end of the semester would come before all of the material was covered. In defense, Grimm argued that the issues that diverted the course were important ones and that one should be free to follow wherever inquiry led. That, after all, is academic freedom, and nobody has the authority to intrude.

Jones had met with Professor Grimm several times on this issue. While rather stubborn and inflexible as an individual, Grimm had always enjoyed a reputation as a sympathetic instructor—concerned enough to meet the students "where they were" and to move ahead only when convinced that all or most were ready. At the last meeting Jones had rather forcefully stated to Grimm that the students were not well served if the class had not prepared them for the third course in the sequence. While Grimm seemed to agree, he could be rather enigmatic, and Jones had no confidence that he would improve.

The issue had become a major one, because students from the department of economics as well as history were involved. This was the second year now that problems had developed, and Jones worried that he was no nearer a solution. The obvious remedies were not available. For instance, no one in the economics department was available to teach the course and Grimm was the only historian who could do it. The dean had frozen the budget for part-time help and, anyway, Jones doubted he could find a qualified person, as the college was located in a remote area. Finally, Grimm was not eligible for sabbatical for another two years.

What are some possibilities for Jones to consider?

Here again the question of academic freedom is raised, and in this case joined with the issue of preferred teaching style. At least two course objectives seem to be in conflict here—meeting students "where they are" and covering all of the material presupposed by the next course in the series. How can Harry

Jones persuade Professor Grimm to change? What other strategies should he consider in attempting to resolve this problem?

Response #1

Harry Jones should continue his forceful course of action
with Professor Grimm. The academic integrity of the American
economic institutions sequence must not be jeopardized, particularly if Grimm does not teach the final course of the
sequence.

Grimm's lame appeal to academic freedom is spurious. Academic freedom means the freedom of a teacher to discuss
social, economic, or political problems without interference
from officials, organized groups, etc. Academic freedom does
not mean the freedom to neglect course subject matter.

What should Jones do? He should keep a record of all his
discussions with Grimm, other staff members, and students
involved in the problem and should so advise Grimm. Inas-
much as Grimm has led Jones to believe that he (Grimm) will
indeed address all the course objectives, Jones must follow up
to see that Grimm performs. Jones should monitor all course
materials and, if necessary, observe classes to ensure the
desired academic integrity. Of course, these actions should be
undertaken with the utmost professional discretion, but
Professor Grimm must be convinced of his chairperson's
resolve to see this matter through. (George Bagwell, Area
Dean/Alpine Campus Director, Colorado Mountain Col-
lege/Alpine Campus, Steamboat Springs, Colorado.)

Bagwell stresses the importance of the chairperson establishing a pattern of consistent behavior with Grimm.
Indeed, the implication is that the chairperson should indicate that a case for dereliction of duty may be established.
Consistent failure to meet course objectives cannot be tol-
erated, and Bagwell counsels a strong role for the chairper-

son. The following response by Susan M. Robison carries the analysis further and indicates some of the other tactics that the chairperson might utilize.

Response #2

There are two aspects of the course-series problem that must be explored to keep Grimm and the rest of the department happy. The first aspect is the needs of the department, and the second is the needs of the instructor. Grimm has put his own needs for the type of class he likes ahead of the needs of the department. A balance must be restored. The two aspects require different methods of attention. The department needs will be met by feedback and suggestions to Grimm about how to meet his responsibility to the student. And Grimm's need will be met by a faculty-development program to help him adapt his teaching techniques to different situations.

Giving negative feedback is probably one of the most difficult tasks of the department chairman. A couple of tips borrowed from business management can make this difficult job easier.

1. State feedback as positively as possible. Rather than telling Grimm what a terrible teacher he is, Jones should tell him how he could improve his course by focusing discussion on the syllabus topics.

2. Be specific. Grimm can teach his course better if he knows exactly what the students and the department are concerned about. He might need to see the results of a survey. He might benefit from having the teacher of the third course in the sequence show him course evaluations with the specific complaints from the students.

3. Suggest that Grimm gather his own information,

through such devices as course evaluations. Informal interviews with students might reveal their dissatisfaction with Grimm's presentation of information, even though they have seemed delighted with class discussion during the course.

Performance feedback can be an opportunity to assess and guide the faculty member in the faculty-development areas. Grimm seems to enjoy discussion and digressions. Perhaps he would benefit from teaching an upper-level or graduate seminar in special topics. He might like to design his courses to allow for more discussion once a week, while the other days would be structured to lecture material. He could reorganize his assignments to grant more responsibility to the students for panels, simulations, and role plays on controversial topics. Grimm could drop in for a visit to a class taught by someone in the department noted for skillfully led discussions. He might experiment with such techniques as taping, videotaping, and keeping class logs to assess how a discussion is going.

Jones could discuss whether Grimm's needs for stimulation are being met. Many college teachers enter the profession because of high needs for intellectual stimulation, and they experience burnout if those needs are not met. Grimm may be trying to meet his intellectual needs with his students instead of in more appropriate ways, such as collaboration with colleagues, involvement in professional organizations, and outside consulting. If Grimm is due for a sabbatical in two years, he could prepare for it by applying for grants and refining his professional goals, seeking out research mentors. If Grimm meets his professional needs appropriately he will be better able to separate his professional goals from the goals for the second economics institutions course. Grimm, the students, and the department will benefit from a conference with an able department chair. (Susan M. Robison, Associate Professor, Psychology Department, College of Notre Dame of Maryland, Baltimore, Maryland.)

C. "The T.A."—Faculty Misuse of Students

Institutions with graduate programs seem sooner or later to encounter problems with teaching and research assistants. Both faculty and students can have unrealistic expectations. Faculty should provide appropriate mentoring and counseling with regard to the work of those assistants they supervise. At the same time, the assistants should provide the faculty with some relief in the areas of assignment. There is ample opportunity for conflict between these two objectives. The following case study illustrates one not uncommon situation.

THE T.A.

The knock on the door was hesitant, almost inaudible. It came at 5:15 in the afternoon, right when Talcott Weber was gathering things for his briefcase in preparation for leaving for the weekend. He wanted very much to ignore it, but duty won out. Cornelius Recht was standing there, apprehension and indecision on his face.

Recht was the teaching assistant for one of the senior professors in the department, Amanda Macky. Macky had acquired a considerable reputation in sociological studies of sex roles in business and was a major figure not only in the department but in the institution as well. Recht, however, was profoundly disillusioned. Far from what he expected, Recht observed, Macky was simply not displaying appropriate professional behavior. Not only did she not keep office hours, but her lectures this year had been obviously unprepared and poorly presented. Undergraduate students had complained to Recht that they had not gotten back their research papers prior to the last major exam, as the syllabus indicated they should. Recht, who was supposed to grade examinations only, was being blamed for Macky's negligence in grading the papers.

When Weber expressed sympathy for the difficulty Recht must feel, the T.A. seemed to relax a bit. Gulping for more air, he added that he didn't wish to appear petty, but that Professor Macky was also making demands that he just didn't have time to handle. For instance, only the week before she had asked him to photocopy some materials for her research. It took him all afternoon—and he was a teaching assistant, not a research assistant. Certainly he shouldn't have to be doing chores for her.

Recht added that he knew that he was late in coming to Dr. Weber, now that they were into final exams. He had put off coming because he did not want to appear a malcontent, nor did he wish to jeopardize his future in the department. For that reason, Recht continued, he hoped that the chairperson could keep his own role in this confidential. Because of Macky's reputation and contacts in the field, he certainly did not want to alienate her.

How should Weber respond to Recht and what strategies should he devise for dealing with Macky?

Chairpersons responsible for extensive graduate programs need to have sound policies for both assigning and monitoring teaching and research assistants. The following response develops this theme.

Response #1

Weber, the chairman of the department, has some clear responsibilities to Recht, the teaching assistant: one is to protect him from Macky's excessive demands on his time, as indicated by her asking the T.A. to photocopy materials for her research, and another is to define clearly for Recht and Macky the duties of a teaching assistant. Whose responsibility was it, for instance, to *grade* and *return* to the students their research papers prior to the last major examination, as the syllabus indicated? Did Recht have an understanding with Macky that he should grade the papers? If this responsibility had been made clear by the chairman in a "contract" with the T.A. and his supervisor, or in a job description for *all* T.A.s, then Recht should not have to assume the blame for not returning the papers to the students.

In dealing with both Recht and Professor Macky, Weber has to be diplomatic. He should not react immediately to

Recht's accusations as though they were true. He should listen, but he should make it clear that he will discuss and clarify the situation with Macky. At the same time, Weber should encourage Recht to continue carrying out any of Macky's assignments that are directly connected with teaching and compliment him on his patience and tact in dealing thus far with the situation. In dealing with Macky, Weber should suggest to her that teaching assistants are expected to perform only those duties that are already defined and that they need their free time for their own studies.

The case of the T.A. indicates that Weber has lost control of a situation involving a senior professor, that problems with Macky are deeper and more serious than those that have surfaced with Recht. The chairman must reestablish himself as the "real" chairman so that he will be able to respond more positively when one of his faculty members is accused of not keeping office hours and of not being adequately prepared for classes. It seems that Professor Macky needs to be rehabilitated and that Professor Weber needs to establish guidelines for both his teachers and his students. If, for example, an evaluative process or system had been devised for the department, Recht and the students of Macky would have had a channel through which to complain or make valuable comments and suggestions concerning the course well before the final examination period. (Estelle W. Taylor, Chairman, English Department, Howard University, Washington, D.C.)

Gathering information is an important step in dealing with any allegation of unsatisfactory performance. Consider how this process is laid out in the following response.

Response #2

Professor Weber should thank Recht for his frank discussion of the problem, assure him that he will be assigned to assist another professor next semester, and dismiss him. Weber then might discreetly interview graduate students who have been teaching assistants under the direction of Professor Macky in the past and review whatever files are available to determine whether: (1) there is a history of such actions on Professor Macky's part, (2) this is the first time such a thing has happened, or (3) Recht's presentation of the case is less than fully accurate.

If (3) is true, a chat with Recht should straighten things out. If (2) is true, Professor Weber might talk informally with Professor Macky in order to indicate his awareness of the problem and to suggest rather firmly that thoroughly professional relations with teaching assistants must be maintained at all times, implying some possible consequences if there should be more of the same complaints.

If (1) is true, the problem is more complex. Depending on its seriousness, Professor Weber might confront Professor Macky with the documented history of her unprofessionalism, file a report with the dean, and take appropriate action. Such action might include greatly reducing his salary recommendations for Professor Macky this year, monitoring her teaching and T.A. supervision more closely in the future, etc.

Professor Macky needs to be taught that academic professionalism includes responsibilities to students (graduate and otherwise) as well as to colleagues and to the scholarly discipline. (Howard Mancing, Associate Professor of Spanish, University of Missouri/Columbia.)

Chairpersons can easily be caught in the conflict between a student's desire for confidentiality and the faculty member's demand to know who is doing the complaining. Sometimes, as in this case, it will be clear who the unhappy student is. In other situations the chairperson must decide how to handle the conflicting requests.

Individuals seem to differ on the value to be attached to confidentiality. One concern is that a request for confidentiality can mask a reluctance to be fully accountable. A countervailing concern is that in most cases the student, rather than the faculty member, is at risk and so, without the protection of confidentiality, is more vulnerable. Of course, some complaints can be addressed only if the student signs a statement, and he or she should be so advised at the outset.

D. "Early Deadwood"—Midcareer Slump

A common concern among chairpersons is how to deal with those department faculty members who have ceased being productive. After tenure has been awarded, productivity sometimes falls off. Research projects can play out, not to be renewed. Course development can slow down, occasionally stopping altogether.

Perhaps because it is like washing dirty linen, the concern is not usually aired publicly by chairpersons. However, it is certainly heard mentioned in discussions among chairpersons themselves. At the very least, tenure is an institutional matter, but unproductive faculty members are the concern of the chairperson.

Such faculty members present a difficult problem that abounds with poignancy. One's hope is that those who are deadwood are really only "dozingwood." How, then, can they be awakened? And what to do with those who will not respond to loud noises and cold washcloths?

"Early Deadwood" suggests the need for faculty-development opportunities, specifically for those individuals who are experiencing early stagnation in their careers. This case also illustrates the problem of reduced resources that might function as incentives to improvement for those who are tenured.

EARLY DEADWOOD

It was clear now that tenuring Loudspeak had been a mistake. At the time, though, it had seemed so reasonable, indeed eminently appropriate. Loudspeak had come to the campus like an angel of deliverance, determined to turn around what had been a badly demoralized music department. And for a

time he succeeded brilliantly. But then with increasing rapidi-
ty his star diminished. And now the department was no better
off than it had been earlier.

Before Loudspeak came, the music department had been
in complete disarray—student enrollment had plummeted
from previous peak years when interest had been sustained
by the popular jazz instructor, since retired. The other instructors were competent enough, but nobody seemed to have any
creative ideas or imagination about new roles the department
could play within the institution.

As brand-new head of the fine arts division at the time,
Aleithea Kala had persuaded the administration that the
music department needed an additional faculty slot. The administration agreed, its favorable disposition helped by a
recent bequest in support of "instruction and performance in
music." The strategy that the college dean and Kala agreed on
was to bring in someone of vigor who could restore the
department to its earlier glory. The position would be advertised nationally, and the search process was to be rigorous.
While the salary was modest, the institution did have certain
attractions, and it was hoped that someone young but with
great promise could be secured.

Leonard Loudspeak soon emerged as a leading candidate.
An assistant professor in his third year of a nonrenewable
three-year appointment at an Ivy League university, Loudspeak was anxious to relocate to a more permanent position.
Upon inquiry from Kala, colleagues at the university gave him
high ratings in both enthusiasm and teaching abilities and his
graduate professors spoke of him as a highly competent
musician.

During his interview at the college, Loudspeak was a great
hit. Students were completely won over and talked with enthusiasm about his coming. Department and division colleagues were impressed by his credentials and his command
of the arts generally. Everyone was taken with his plans for
organizing an annual folk music festival and a first-rate
college jazz band. While definitely ambitious, the plans
sounded feasible.

The decision to hire him was an easy one, and Loudspeak
came in the fall as associate professor of music and director of

both the jazz band and the folk festival. He was a bit more expensive than the college had hoped, but the president willingly signed the contract. That was three years ago.

The first year, the extra expense needed to hire Loudspeak seemed quite worth it. Students flocked to his courses in music appreciation and the history of American folk music. The jazz band was organized, and its two concerts were smash successes. The first folk festival was widely hailed and gave the college good regional publicity. Pleased with his successes, the college awarded Loudspeak tenure and gave him a substantial merit award. Kala supported these actions. Indeed, she had initiated them.

How fickle people could be, she came to realize. The very next year the first of the student complaints had come. "Professor Loudspeak's success has gone to his head," several of the senior students said. "Last year he was terrific, but this year he's just a bully." Students from other classes of his made similar comments. At the annual evaluation session, Kala questioned Loudspeak about these comments but was told that it was simply his effort to increase standards that the students resented.

By the middle of Loudspeak's third year, however, the student complaints had increased substantially. The second folk festival was a disappointment. Loudspeak's division colleagues had started to mutter about him, charging that he was arrogant and difficult to work with—indeed, that these flaws of his were the reasons for the lackluster festival. Some also hinted that he was ridiculing their own classes before students. Kala talked with Loudspeak again about these issues. Again, though, she was informed of his efforts to increase standards. Faculty colleagues, Loudspeak contended, must resent his leadership. They were also probably jealous of his high salary, he added. As for the festival, other colleges were now offering them, and the public's interests seemed to have peaked.

What are the options Kala has now with regard to Loudspeak? How should she proceed?

Other issues that can be explored include: How can the division head persuade Loudspeak to confront more honestly the character of his relationships with other division faculty? Taking into account the significant deterioration in Loudspeak's performance, should a reduction in his salary or rank be threatened? As departments increasingly experience lesser turnover and older average faculty ages, how can the performance of the tenured faculty be monitored? What are good, workable early-warning systems?

Response #1

Loudspeak is tenured, so Kala must work with what she has. She should consider the following actions.

First, she should identify the real problem. It appears to be a mix of jealousy on the part of other faculty members and arrogance on Loudspeak's part. It would be important to determine the actual proportions involved. She might, for instance, schedule head-to-head sessions with the other faculty members to get their perspectives, both individually and as a group. She should have a similar meeting with Loudspeak. She might also try having both of these meetings with an outside consultant.

Once the problem is better defined, Kala should explore the use of a facilitator to try to persuade the two factions to listen to each other. They need to share information and to communicate concerns in a positive manner. The facilitator should point out that they will have to work with each other for some time to come.

Kala does need to lead the division to some common understanding and agreement on appropriate standards. Such an understanding would function as a bench mark against which to gauge what are unacceptably "high" standards.

Finally, Kala should consider devising a new project for Loudspeak. (Lester L. Rosenbloom, Chairman, Business Administration Division, Corning Community College, Corning, New York.)

This response draws our attention to the importance of the

department or division as a whole dealing with the issue. Rarely is one person a problem without others contributing or assisting in some way. The second response argues for the importance of a supportive stance by Kala, since further alienating Loudspeak can have few positive results.

Response #2

Kala has relatively few options with regard to Loudspeak, since he has already been awarded tenure. There are, however, some courses of action open to her. She can "write off her losses"—that is, rationalize the current situation as not significantly worse than it was before Loudspeak came and hope that over time Loudspeak will tone down and begin again to make a positive contribution to the department. She can continue to try to talk with Loudspeak about student and colleague dissatisfaction, hoping that eventually the persistence of the complaints will make an impact. She can warn Loudspeak that future salary increases and the possibility of promotion to full professor will be significantly reduced if student and colleague dissatisfaction persists. A fourth option would be a combination of these approaches.

Writing off Loudspeak and hoping for the best is a strategy that requires little effort by Kala but also has little chance of a satisfactory long-range solution for either Loudspeak or for the department. The warning approach alone has the advantage of making quite clear to Loudspeak the probable consequence of continuing his present course but runs the risk of making him even more defensive. Loudspeak may end up lumping Kala in with those faculty colleagues who, he contends, "must resent his leadership." Further discussions with Loudspeak may pay off, but this action seems insufficient in and of itself, since several previous conversations have not led to any significant changes.

The option with the greatest chance of success is probably a series of conversations with Loudspeak, which would begin with Kala's statement about the likely professional consequences of Loudspeak's current behavior. The discussion should proceed by Kala's indicating an appreciation of the difficulties of the position that Loudspeak was hired to assume. She should make Loudspeak aware that when he was hired, everyone, including herself, had unrealistic expectations that he would "restore the department to its earlier glory," an enormous burden to lay on any individual. Those expectations were also made quite clear to Loudspeak when he was hired at a higher salary than the college had at first counted on. Loudspeak did appear to live up to those unreasonable expectations during the first year, but it is difficult for anyone to continue to perform at that level. Disappointment was inevitable. Loudspeak reacted to that disappointment in a defensive manner, trying to rationalize his "failure" to be a superman in terms of students' desires to be pampered and collegial jealousy.

Kala's indicating an understanding of Loudspeak's feelings may be sufficient for Loudspeak to consider her "on his side" and thus be more open to suggestions about change. Kala should offer Loudspeak personal and colleague support in organizing another folk festival, suggesting perhaps that students also be involved. She should somehow get across to Loudspeak that it is not too late to regain the confidence of those who brought him to the college and that changing his style and asking for assistance rather than becoming defensive and resentful about having to do it alone is likely to pay off for him both personally and professionally. She should also underscore her readiness to be helpful and work *with him* to reestablish the music department's position within the college. (Harriett G. Tolpin, Chairperson, Simmons College, Boston, Massachusetts.)

E. "Senior Deadwood"—A Growing Problem

A complicating factor in the current increase in the average age of department and division faculty is the recent congressional prohibition of mandatory retirement before the age of seventy. For higher education the prohibition took effect in July of 1982 and can throw into turmoil the faculty staffing plans of many institutions. "Senior Deadwood" illustrates some of the problems that can develop.

SENIOR DEADWOOD

For several years both the arts and sciences dean and the department chairperson had taken comfort from the approaching retirement of Bill Kirkwood. Once a vigorous researcher and teacher with a good regional reputation, Kirkwood had become increasingly inactive in the past decade. Tenured and promoted to full professor years ago, he was still physically robust. Mentally he seemed alert enough, but his determination to take on large projects had weakened noticeably.

Much earlier, students had come to the department in order to study with him. Now he was widely regarded as out of date and considered to be merely coasting. In addition, his area of expertise, art education, had fallen into shadow as the surplus of secondary teachers had taken hold. Kirkwood had developed no new interests, however. His contributions to the department and to scholarship had also fallen off, and he had long since ceased pulling his weight in committee work and student advising.

It was bad enough that he had ceased to be productive. Worse yet, he was now handicapping others. Always a talkative person, his garrulousness was proving an affliction to colleagues. People would flee when they heard him coming. He would do his best to pursue them, though, talking as he went.

Nevertheless, people felt some strange affection for him. At least, and perhaps more accurately, no one was willing to be sufficiently abrupt or rude. Everyone simply looked forward to his retirement the following year. Therefore it came as a shock to Clyde, the art department's chairperson, when Kirkwood indicated recently that he was reconsidering his retirement plans.

He didn't wish to leave the department in a lurch, Kirkwood explained, nor did he wish to disappoint the students who had come to the department because he was there. Besides, Kirkwood added, he felt that he needed something to do. When Clyde registered his surprise at this development and indicated that it would create difficulties for the department, Kirkwood responded that he was simply exercising his rights under the new legislation prohibiting mandatory retirement policies prior to age seventy. Furthermore, Kirkwood added, because of his seniority, he felt entitled to continue offering the courses he did so well.

Mercifully, Kirkwood left the office soon afterward, leaving Clyde to ponder what he could do. The prospect of more years of Kirkwood was in itself a heavy blow. His continuation also had serious consequences for the department curriculum. The financial condition of the institution meant that no further slots could be envisioned for the department. The curriculum committee had for several years been stymied in developing the new direction it felt necessary—stymied because courses had to be dropped in order to make room for the new ones. Kirkwood's area was the logical choice, but his inability to teach in other areas meant little possibility of movement.

Of course, Clyde thought to himself, Kirkwood could simply be assigned different courses. He would then either sink or swim. If by some miracle he did swim, then the department could move on ahead with its new curricular plans. It was more likely, however, that he would simply sink—thereby solving no one's problems. In any case, giving Kirkwood greater prominence in the curriculum would mean afflicting him on more of the students. And that, in turn, could well drive some of them away and those that remained would hardly be well-served.

On the other hand, those students in his present courses were hardly being well-served either. There was little prospect that Clyde could see that their fortunes would improve. Short of putting out a contract on Kirkwood, Clyde thought ruefully, the department and its students seemed locked into one of two unpleasant possibilities—continuing the status quo or terminating Kirkwood for cause. Are there other alternatives that Clyde is overlooking? What strategies should he pursue?

Clyde could initiate steps to relieve Kirkwood of his position, citing either incompetence or program redirection. Either case would require consultation with the dean and very careful preparation. The two procedures should not be confused, although both could be used here. Alternatively, Clyde might propose to Kirkwood a part-time work arrangement. However, if Kirkwood is motivated at least in part by financial concerns, he will likely resist the proposal.

Many senior professors remain very productive, of course, but even they may create staffing difficulties for the department as they delay their retirement plans. Kirkwood's case presents a severe challenge to both planning and performance counseling. Consider the following responses:

Response #1

Amendments to the Age Discrimination in Employment Act (ADEA), which became effective in 1978 and subsequently raised the minimum retirement age from age sixty-five to seventy, temporarily exempted tenured college and university faculty. Unfortunately for Clyde and the department of art, that special exemption expired at the end of June 1982. Assuming the Kirkwood reached his institution's mandatory retirement age after that date, he is correct in asserting his rights to continued employment to age seventy under the provisions of the act as amended. The prospect of his continuation, however, only confirms the negative consequences of the act envisioned by higher-education administrators when they urged adoption of the special exemption in 1978: decline of faculty vitality, outdated curricula, steadily increasing staffing costs. The four-year exemption period was granted in order to allow institutions with a mandatory retirement age lower than seventy time to design innovative early or phased-retirement policies or, at the very least, time to examine the long-range implications of ADEA policy on institutional staffing. Had Kirkwood's institution taken aggressive advantage of this opportunity to develop overall institutional policy, then the department of art might not be facing the current problem.

It is unfortunately the case that retirement plans conceived of in more favorable economic periods must be reconsidered in periods of high inflation. Although Kirkwood publicly cites one set of concerns for his decision to forego retirement at this time, his private concerns might well be more economic than otherwise. It is Clyde's responsibility as chairman to determine Kirkwood's actual motives.

If it appears that Kirkwood is sincere in thinking that his retirement will leave the department in dire circumstances, then Clyde's job is going to be much more difficult and painful, since he must in some way correct Kirkwood's distorted perceptions of his value as a teacher, scholar, and colleague. One way for the department to accomplish this would be to adopt a policy of uniformly evaluating all members of the department, tenured and untenured, in the several areas of faculty productivity. One dislikes being too devious in such matters, but adoption of such a policy would likely be good for everyone and might create an effective disincentive for Kirkwood to continue teaching.

Whatever the department decides about evaluation, curricular redesign that has been delayed pending Kirkwood's retirement must go forward. It seems immaterial whether Kirkwood is teaching poorly in a new program or teaching poorly in an old one, and at least the other members of the department will be engaged in teaching what they consider to be a more appropriate and timely curriculum. That Kirkwood is a likely candidate for rejuvenation through some form of faculty redevelopment seems doubtful, although that strategy should not be discounted altogether. The cost in department morale of simply waiting out Kirkwood's second projected retirement is something no department can afford. Pursuit of almost any proactive policy in this case is better than simple acquiescence.

On the other hand, if Clyde discovers that Kirkwood's motives for delaying his retirement are based on financial considerations, then the possibility of interesting him in a program of early or phased retirement almost certainly exists. The fact that no overall institutional policy exists does not mean that specific terms cannot be negotiated on an individual basis.

Such action would of course require the full support of the central administration, and no negotiations should begin until all parties have familiarized themselves with the many plans already in force at various insitutions, both public and private. Terms arrived at in Kirkwood's case may well serve as a useful model for future negotiations designed to be mutually beneficial, both to the individual and to the institution. (John Feaster, Associate Dean, College of Arts and Sciences, Valparaiso University, Valparaiso, Indiana.)

Response #2

The first thing that Clyde should recognize is that this is not merely his problem or even his department's problem—it is a dilemma for the arts and sciences college and the whole institution as well. Conditions outside the university—the surplus of secondary teachers—and the need for curriculum revision within the department together suggest the need for change in the department's orientation. The dean has provided at least implicit recognition of this by his taking comfort in Kirkwood's approaching retirement. The implication is that Clyde should not attempt to solve this dilemma within the department and without appeal to the dean and central administration.

One line of inquiry should be the legislation prohibiting mandatory retirement prior to age seventy. He should consult the university attorney to determine what the institution's policy is in complying with the legislation. Does the law specify that the employee must be retained in the same position (i.e., teaching the same course, as Kirkwood suggests), or are reassignments permissible? Has the university developed a "golden handshake" policy to encourage early retirement or reassignment?

Depending upon what Clyde finds here, his strategy should be to seek institutional support for relieving Kirkwood of his present teaching duties. Kirkwood must be: (1) reassigned to a nonteaching post elsewhere in the university, (2) reassigned to other duties within the department with the institution underwriting the cost of this shift, or (3) given the financial incentive to reconsider the extension of his appointment.

The case Clyde constructs should be broadly based, considering not merely the implications of Kirkwood's continued teaching for the department and its students, but also demonstrating the changing external conditions and the need for change in the department's mission that make a shift in assignments imperative.

What this dilemma illustrates is the need for effective performance counseling, even with tenured full professors of academic note. Kirkwood seems unaware of—or unwilling to face—the devaluation of his performance and his decreasing importance to the department in recent years. This should have been documented and communicated to him and the administration in the decade during which he became increasingly inactive and a handicap to others in the department. It seems cruel and insensitive to spring it on him at this point in his career. If the administration will not face the obvious and respond positively to Clyde's entreaties, he and his department simply will have to invest in earplugs. (Walter B. Jaehnig, Head, Journalism and Telecommunication Department, University of Wyoming, Laramie, Wyoming.)

Of course, there are many other situations within a department that can call for performance counseling. Individuals can perform unsatisfactorily in regard to research as well as teaching. They can be inadequate in student advising or in general institutional service. Each of these situations will be different and will require a different approach. Common to all, however, will be the need for regular contact, the communication of a clear understanding of expectations, and agreement on a timetable for achieving them.

A common lament of chairpersons is the diminished time available to them for teaching and research. Because of their own slipping research productivity or instructional zing, many chairpersons may feel awkward or at a disadvantage in counseling others with inadequate records. This provides all the more reason to move the department as a whole toward a common understanding of appropriate standards and expectations—the topic of the next chapter.

CHAPTER FIVE

Departmental Goals, Change, and Decision Making

DEALING WITH UNSATISFACTORY PERFORMANCE and resolving conflicts usually require some prior clarity and consensus about basic department objectives. The department, after all, is a fundamental organizational unit. It is more than simply an aggregation of individuals with different personal agendas and objectives. There must be some common understanding about professional standards and institutional expectations, and some common agreement about the department's directions, obligations, and burdens.

Achieving reasonable clarity and consensus about these departmental objectives can be no mean feat. Faculty members are naturally most concerned about their own individual courses, research projects, and advising loads. As a result, the chairperson needs to create a context and set of circumstances in which the faculty see their own individual goals as achieved through meeting the department goals. In effect, the chairperson needs to give breath and spirit to what is otherwise simply a slot on an organizational chart. A department understood simply as an aggregation of individuals has insufficient unity. Some faculty members may cite the Adam Smith principle—that the welfare of the whole is inevitably advanced when each part or member simply pursues his own individual interest. However, it is the rare department that can function effectively under these circumstances. The job of the chair is to create the department out of these individuals.

As far as broad objectives are concerned, this is easily done. Thus, all but the truly dumb or the few with independent incomes will see their economic fortunes to be tied up with those of the department and the institution. The difficulties come in forging a common understanding of what specifically the department should be doing in regard to such matters as curricular thrust, grading standards, admission and graduation requirements, staffing, student recruiting, and off-campus courses. Yet it is precisely such understandings that constitute the cement or glue that bonds the department.

These problems have become more challenging recently, as institutions are forced to respond to inflation and to social shifts in educational interests, values, and needs. Certainly demographic changes are pressing institutions to reexamine their goals and policies, as well as student involvement in these matters. The reality of decreased federal and state support for public and private institutions alike compounds the challenge.

As the institution adjusts to its changing environment, the department must determine that its own particular mission is appropriate and viable. In all of this, of course, the department must be constantly concerned that it stay abreast of developments in the discipline. And it is the chairperson who is responsible for engineering or coordinating these changes. The following case studies illustrate some of the problems involved.

A. "Grading Practices at Old Ford Community College"—Dealing with Extremes

Establishing and maintaining reasonably unified department practices on even fairly ordinary matters can sometimes be a major challenge for the chairperson. Among the practices that the chairperson may need to keep a close eye on is grading and other measures of student performance. The case study "Grading Practices at Old Ford Community College" illustrates some of the difficulties that can emerge.

GRADING PRACTICES AT OLD FORD COMMUNITY COLLEGE

The joys of the division were not all they were cracked up to be, thought Dr. Black. Why anyone would want to be a chair for ten years, as his predecessor had, was utterly beyond him. His own three years would be more than enough—if he survived them!

One reason for this mood had just left. Dr. Largess was a tenured associate professor in the department. He had once been a rather quiet person who carried out his responsibilities with a minimum of fanfare and delay. For some reason, however, he had changed in the last couple of years. Perhaps his divorce had played a role. In any case, Largess had radically changed his grading practice, and Black was concerned.

Black had always thought that there was a tacit understanding within the profession, a sort of gentlemen's agreement, about grading. Rigid adherence to a bell-shaped grade-distribution curve was ridiculous, of course, but so was giving out almost all A's in a class of thirty-five. Yet that was exactly what Professor Largess had now done for two semesters in a row in American History 101.

The first time this happened, Black asked Largess about

the student performance in the class. "Top-notch," was the response, "the best ever." Perhaps three fourths of them had deserved A's, Black reflected, so he did not pursue the issue further.

But now it had happened again. Only this time four fifths of the students had received A's. Black was concerned. He did not want the department to get a reputation for offering easy courses. On the other hand, he did not want to violate academic freedom or professional judgment. He did not like confrontations, and he was afraid that Largess might become defensive if the issue was put on the next department meeting agenda. However, the brief report of department grade distribution he had circulated toward the end of the last semester had clearly not had its desired effect.

It would be good to get out of this mess, Black said to himself. His first and best love, teaching, had been neglected too long. But he did have one more year as chair, and he was determined to leave affairs in good shape. How should he proceed with Largess? What options does he have, and what strategies should he develop?

Among the issues that can be discussed: What ways are there for securing a unified department philosophy on grading, assuming there should be one, and for ensuring adherence to it? How can one be reasonably certain that grades are appropriate? What strategies can one adopt with the occasional individualist who marches to an entirely different drum beat? Do strategies need to be different for dealing with those who grade too stringently? The following responses deal with some of these issues.

Response #1

Dr. Black is concerned that Largess is disregarding the importance of grading. To give all of the students A's is to prepare them poorly for further coursework. An easy A also suggests to the students that the profession is an easy mark for success, whereas it is probably very competitive. It is important, then, that Largess realize that his permissive grading may begin a series of many actions requiring many more interventions.

Not only has Largess not represented the true vigor of the professional demands expected in his academic area, but he has misled the students and has tarnished the academic image of the department. Black should confront Largess in an indirect manner in several department conversations dealing with issues relating directly to the professional expectations of graduates in the career area and the image of the department in the academic community. For instance, these items could be on the agenda of the next faculty meeting. In each of these conversations the focus would be on the larger issue rather than grade distribution.

After Largess has participated in these general discussions, Black could speak to him privately and review the impact of his grading on his students' careers and the department's image. Black should point out that he does not expect a formula distribution but does expect that students be given a realistic report on their mastery of the subject area. (Jim Raughton, Division Director, Science and Technology Division, Community College of Denver, Denver, Colorado.)

Response #2

It appears that Black does not enjoy being chair and will probably only serve out the remaining year of his term. If this is true, he may not have been conducting regular performance-counseling interviews with his department colleagues. However, before leaving office, he might wish to initiate a conference of an informal nature with each of his colleagues to review matters during his three-year term of office. In such a conference he might review the accomplishments of each faculty member, examine strengths and weaknesses in performance, discuss the faculty member's hopes, aspirations, and professional goals, and examine the present and future goals of the department.

Black should try to learn all he can about Largess before they meet. There may be some personal reason why Largess' grading habits have changed. Largess may be in a state of personal crisis as a result of his divorce. During the discussion Black should show a genuine interest in Largess. However, he should be direct and honest with him. Black should be clear in pointing out that the department has criteria, standards, a "gentlemen's agreement" in regard to grading and that Largess' latest grading habits are not acceptable. Black should try to create an environment in which Largess can be free to speak about his difficulty. If the problem is the divorce adjustment, is there something Black or colleagues in the department can do to help? Does Largess feel tired? Burned out? Would a change in assignment help? Largess might be asked to think about this and meet again with Black in a few weeks to decide on a course of action.

Alternatively, Black could put the matter of evaluation of students on the department agenda. For the meeting, he could have prepared historical data on grading patterns of each faculty member. Historical data on the overall grading patterns of the community college by department might also be available for faculty in comparing their department with others. A discussion can ensue about faculty members' differing evaluation methods and resulting grading patterns. The department's criteria and standards on the matter should be reviewed and compared with other departments. Hopefully, an open discussion on the topic might encourage a positive change in Largess. (Toni Iadorola, Provost, College of Mount St. Joseph on the Ohio, Mount St. Joseph, Ohio.)

Response #3

Black will undoubtedly want to do some consulting with his colleagues before taking any action. He needs to discuss the matter with Largess, but he will be in a much better position to represent the department and to defend himself—in the event that discussion turns to confrontation—if he can cite the opinions of his colleagues.

Grading is a sacred matter, and most departments are willing to tolerate idiosyncracies even though erratic grading can produce injustices and undermine a department's reputation. It is therefore likely that Black's colleagues will suggest a moderate approach. Black should then enter into his conversation with Largess with the attitude that Largess has the right to give all A's if he wishes. Black will of course point out the injustice to students and the effects of such a grading policy on the credibility of the department.

It is possible that Black's colleagues will advocate a strong stance against Largess' apparent dilution of department standards. If this is the case, Black must be willing to present the department's position clearly and objectively. He obviously doesn't have much stomach for it, but he should try to convince himself that whatever the outcome he will have done his duty and earned the respect and gratitude of his colleagues. He must recognize that he probably cannot force a change in Largess' grading policy, since arbitrary grading is certainly not grounds for dismissal of a tenured faculty member. He should make clear in his presentation that he is not threatening Largess, but is rather seeking voluntary compliance with department standards.

In either case, a low-key conversation in which Black indicates respect for Largess' individuality will at least ease Black's conscience about his neglected responsibility; and there are reasonable expectations that it may do much more. Largess may be unaware that he is out of step with the department and perhaps with reality. He may change his grading policy. Futhermore, it is not beyond hope that a sincere interest on the part of Black in Largess' grading philosophy and academic standards may lead to a frank, personal exchange that would explain Largess' apparent behavior change.

Black really has nothing to lose—except perhaps a night's sleep preceding his conversation with Largess—if he is prepared to accept Largess' refusal to change his present grading policy; and the possibilities of a positive outcome are excellent. (Paul J. Schwartz, Chairman, Department of Modern and Classical Languages, University of North Dakota, Grand Forks, North Dakota.)

Securing a department consensus about grading policies for students is an important part of the glue that actually bonds or creates the *one* department. Another part of this glue is the generation of a common set of assumptions about faculty evaluation. Every chairperson must promote the concept and practice of responsible peer evaluation. Because grading practices will be part of the colleague assessment, a strong departmental practice of peer evaluation will also have an impact on student evaluation.

B.   "Schedule Equity"—Distributing the Burdens

Department chairpersons frequently worry about the problem of maintaining equity in distributing department burdens. Obvious and traditional problems include establishing parity between lecture and laboratory assignments, constructing fair policies on research efforts and course overloads, and dealing with independent-study involvements. Advising loads are another issue. Course scheduling is a special problem for many chairpersons, especially with regard to the less attractive class hours. "Schedule Equity" illustrates a common difficulty in handling this problem.

SCHEDULE EQUITY

Sarah found herself facing the same scheduling conundrum again. In each of the past four terms she had been chairperson, the staffing of the early-morning classes had been a problem. Eight o'clock was not an especially attractive time, and two faculty members of the nine-member department were aggravating the problem.

One, Jim Stuart, was an instructor who was still working on his doctoral degree at Bottom University sixty miles away.

He had two more classes to complete. For both this term and the next he had to be at Bottom each Monday and Wednesday morning.

The other, Mary White, had completed her terminal degree before coming to the department. However, she had started her family several years ago and, now that she was a single parent, had found appropriate child-care arrangements to be a problem. In particular, she claimed to be unable to accept early-morning classes and still take care of her family.

The other members of the department had been understanding at the beginning. Some grumbling was beginning to develop, however. Indeed, one of the department members had complained twice now about the uneven distribution of burdens. Sarah herself felt that there was a problem of equity involved. She wondered what was appropriate under the circumstances.

On the one hand, the two faculty members did have special problems that the others did not. On the other hand, they were professionals by choice and as such should be prepared to pull their full weight.

After all, the other members of the department had come with the terminal degree already completed at their own expense. It hardly seemed fair to them in effect to support Stuart when he, too, was on the payroll. Likewise, Mary White's situation was certainly unfortunate, but was it reasonable to ask the other department members always to compensate for it?

The problem seemed to be getting worse, for the two had been neglecting committee assignments recently, using as an excuse their other responsibilities. And then Sarah heard that the new college dean wanted to institute a long-range plan involving night and weekend classes. She certainly couldn't face the challenges that they would bring if the present ones were still unresolved.

Is it time now to establish some principles? What options does Sarah have and how should she pursue them?

Among the issues here: What special responsibilities does a department have to individuals with ongoing personal or family difficulties? For how long is it reasonable to make adjustments and exceptions? Does the department really owe anything to individuals like Jim Stuart? What is the best way to plan for distributing the possible night and weekend teaching assignments? Consider the following responses.

Response #1

Sarah's course of action in this matter is clear. By proceeding in the following ways, she will establish principles of schedule equity that will serve her department well over the long haul.

1. Jim Stuart will be allowed to finish the doctorate, as this is in the best interests of the department. However, he will teach the morning classes the following year.

2. Mary White will take her turn with the morning classes this year. Child-care arrangements are her personal concern, not the concern of the department.

3. All committee assignments will be distributed equitably. Considerations of different teaching loads may be made, but all salaried faculty will assume appropriate committee responsibilities.

4. All salaried faculty will be advised of the dean's long-range plans for night and weekend classes. Sarah should encourage the dean to involve faculty in this planning.

Sarah must be perceived by her faculty as a chairperson who practices fair play now, so that she will have their full cooperation in the future. (George Bagwell, Area Dean/Alpine Campus Director, Colorado Mountain College/Alpine Campus, Steamboat Springs, Colorado.)

Response #2

Apparently two young faculty members in this department are using personal circumstances as an excuse to avoid assuming the full duties of their positions. For a short time this is tolerable. Soon, however, this behavior becomes irresponsible, unprofessional, and also manipulative.

Because departmental morale is being adversely affected and there is no immediate end in sight to the problems of the lax department members, the chairperson needs to make some policy changes immediately. If she does not, she can justly be accused of playing favorites.

Unpopular class times can be rotated, eliminated, assigned to junior faculty, or taught by part-time lecturers in an understaffed department. If rotation is the only feasible alternative, then it should be a department policy that teaching assignments are made fairly. This means that the chairperson gets a turn, too. Consequently, no one becomes overburdened with successive semesters of classes at 8:00 in the morning, or evening classes.

The chairperson should present the unpopular schedules to Mary and Jim with as much advance notice as possible. Her manner should be sympathetic but firm. Personal problems that seem unsolvable frequently work themselves out when alternatives must be actively sought. Perhaps Jim will take a semester's leave of absence to finish his degree. Maybe it will be possible for him to teach half-time with a reduced salary for the troublesome semester. Virtually every employed mother of young children has child-care difficulties. Mary may be forced to explore alternative arrangements that she did not have the incentive to consider seriously before. Above all, the chairperson must be fair and avoid giving the faculty reason to waste time comparing and complaining about the inequities in scheduling.

This problem might have been prevented if the chairperson had made the teaching requirements of the department absolutely clear to new faculty members *before* they were hired. Sarah can learn from her mistakes. (Elizabeth V. Swenson, Associate Professor and Chairperson, Department of Psychology, John Carroll University, Cleveland, Ohio.)

Broader course-assignment issues include dealing with the problem of territoriality, of individuals who perceive certain courses as their own. A special version of this is the academic dean or other administrator who is a part-time member of the department and who stakes out certain courses or times or classrooms as nonnegotiably his or hers. Rotation is one solution, but is a rigorously enforced policy of course rotation necessarily the best use of department resources? Chairpersons will need to make this decision in the context of the particular strengths of their departments.

Many chairs will be tempted to lead by example and will personally assign themselves the unattractive department tasks before asking others to undertake them. This is both a noble and effective leadership style, but it can exact a heavy toll on the chair's time and energy. It is not recommended as a regular practice. Some departments face the difficulties presented by off-campus "centers" to which they are expected to provide an occasional course. Such a contribution may be sufficiently infrequent that it is not a regular department burden. In such cases the chairperson can use the following incentives and rewards for those who serve: reduction in course load, special schedule or course-selection prerogatives, reduced class size, and extra money.

Finally, departments may face equity issues with traditional policies designed to provide special benefits to senior faculty. Since such benefits as reduced course loads are usually awarded regardless of demonstrated merit or desert by the individuals so favored, these policies can appear to those not included to be based simply on longevity. Perhaps they are to compensate for reduced vigor or mental powers! Chairpersons may wish to explore alternative procedures for distributing reduced teaching loads. Perhaps individuals could make application to a department committee, indicating both the reason why the reduction is appropriate and how the additional time will be spent. Certainly such reductions could be an important element in rewarding those who make especially significant contributions or who take risks in introducing innovations.

C. "Eastern University"—Reduction in Size

It is important to secure reasonably uniform department policies and practices on grading and on expectations of student performance generally. Likewise, establishing acceptable and fair policies on distributing department burdens is essential to the health and harmony of the department. However, it is equally essential to be timely in confronting the need to alter the department curriculum or staffing patterns. Certainly a reduction in faculty size is more than a passing prospect to many chairpersons today, particularly those in the "undersubscribed" areas. "Eastern University" presents the dilemma facing one such individual—Tobias Tongue, chairperson of foreign languages.

EASTERN UNIVERSITY

Eastern University is a medium-sized, state-supported institution located in the heart of a large metropolitan area. Originally a liberal arts institution, it was in its ninth decade and served largely an adult population when the department of foreign languages was chaired by Dr. Tobias Tongue, a full professor of Latin. Because of Eastern's origins as a liberal arts institution, courses in both Greek and Latin were offered. Modern languages were also taught, with courses offered in French, Italian, German, and Spanish. There was a two-semester foreign-language course requirement for graduation.

Because of the composition of the surrounding urban community (with a heavy Hispanic population), student demand in the department leaned heavily toward Spanish language and literature. There was only slight interest in the classical offerings. Student enrollment in German had been stable over the years, but interest in French had fallen significantly. Enrollment in Italian had declined even more.

The department was heavily tenured, reflecting the fact that most of the faculty was middle-aged. In fact, only the two assistant professors of Spanish were on probationary appointments. Yet none of the faculty seemed ready to retire, the oldest being only fifty-nine. While Eastern had once had a mandatory retirement age of sixty-five, the federal extension of the retirement age muddied the prospective staffing picture.

The department's decline in student interest and the static character of its faculty were matters of serious concern to Dr. Tongue. In fact, Eastern overall had been experiencing large recent enrollment declines—totaling 16 percent over the past two years. In the first year the university was able to avoid cuts in support. However, the state used an enrollment-based formula and the reductions were later translated into decreased appropriations. Indeed, the university had just received word that state support would be reduced by 6 percent in the next fiscal year.

This unwelcome news was quickly passed around the Eastern grapevine. For some time Dr. Tongue had worried that his department was vulnerable to reduction. This news only heightened his concern.

Since the overwhelming number of students were commuters, they were not well-organized as a group. However, everyone seemed opposed to the idea of any increase in student fees to compensate for reduced state support. In addition, the student newspaper recently ran several articles and editorials calling for a solution of the budget problem through cuts in administration and in deadwood faculty.

Additionally, the militant head of the nonfaculty employee union publicly stated within the past month that the staff was prepared to strike if it did not receive substantial raises. The union leader noted that there were some faculty members who taught only a handful of students a year and that faculty salaries were taking away from funds that should have been going to the overworked support staff. The union head mentioned no names, but Dr. Tongue felt that his department was singularly conspicuous.

Listening to the talk in the faculty lounge, Dr. Tongue gathered that most of his colleagues had little sympathy with the employee union complaints. Nor was there much opposition to an increase in student fees, especially if that was the price for avoiding reductions in the size of the faculty. However, much of the talk in the lounge came down to the ringing declamations by a few that if any layoffs were really necessary there was more than enough fat in the administrative staff. Dr.

Tongue regarded such talk as cheap and feared that real trouble was headed his way.

Other faculty members in his department had also been concerned by the situation. For two years the department had tried to secure greater demand and activity for the department's non-Spanish offerings, but these efforts met with only modest results. For example, efforts were made to promote to other departments the idea of language minors for their majors. Language credentials, the department argued, would enhance the attractiveness of students to future employees. However, students did not display much interest in the idea. Also it was not clear how vigorously the other departments were promoting the concept.

The department members also revived the various language clubs and provided the student members with considerable personal attention. A few faculty members grumbled about pandering to students, but overall the effort was conscientious and sincere. Department members also addressed various student groups on the joys of language study and competency, but attendance at these sessions was usually sparse.

In addition, the department pressed the undergraduate curriculum committee for an increase in the foreign-language requirements for graduation. The proposal went nowhere, however. Dr. Tongue suspected that other faculty members, including those on the curriculum committee, were concerned that any increase in requirements would drive away students.

All of these concerns came to a quick head when Dr. Tongue received a letter from the dean of arts and sciences requesting a meeting to discuss the "staffing situation" in the department. The letter reviewed the general institutional situation with regard to the decrease in state appropriations for the coming year and the various competing claims upon these funds. It then went on to characterize the low level of student demand for language courses as a matter of extreme concern. It also noted the high cost per student credit hour—a function of the expense of the language laboratory and the low enrollments. Finally, the letter requested that the chairperson come prepared to present proposals for reducing the level of department expense by 10 percent and by 20 percent.

How should Dr. Tongue respond to the dean? What should

he say to the students and faculty who have already been stopping him in the hallways asking about the rumors circulating that languages will be cut?

FIGURE 5.1   Department Staff

Spanish

   1 associate professor
   2 assistant professors

Latin and Greek

   2 full professors

French

   1 associate professor
   2 part-time lecturers

German

   2 associate professors

Italian

   1 full professor
   1 part-time lecturer

This department has already pursued several avenues in an effort to increase student interest in its offerings. Are there other possibilities that have not been identified? When no voluntary retirements or departures are in sight, how should a department chairperson plan for a reduction in staff? How far in advance should plans be made for staff reduction, keeping in mind that circumstances can change? How can chairs avoid charges of bias with regard to their own position? In this particular case study, how should Tongue proceed in responding to the dean? And what can be done to avoid self-fulfilling prophecies and a vicious downward spiral for departments in trouble? Consider the following three responses.

Response #1

Several data-based or information items should already have been compiled by the chairman. If nothing has been done, then the following data must be gathered and documented. This information should include data from institutions that are *very similar* to Eastern University.

1. The exact amount of student credit-hour generation in each language area for the past five years.

2. The cost of teaching each course in dollars per FTE or dollars per student credit hour; the cost of maintaining a language laboratory.

3. The graduation requirements, specifically in languages, in effect at other insitutions. Do requirements total more or less than that at Eastern? Are enrollment trends similar to, or different from, those at Eastern?

4. The amount spent for traditionally high-cost programs at Eastern such as physics, chemistry, computer science, etc. Also a cost figure regarding the running of laboratories required in these programs.

5. Staffing formulas or policies regarding support-staff positions and salaries. This information may be critical in dealing with this problem.

6. The amount of money that students are paying in fees and tuition to take a comparable load. Is an increase planned? If so, how much and in what areas?

Dr. Tongue should already have been deeply involved in staff development or retrenchment plans. If none exists, Eastern is remiss as an institution. Points in the plan should include the following:

1. Are sabbatical leaves available in the immediate future? Faculty members may have to exercise this option to retrain.

2. Is the option of teaching part-time during the summer session available? This in turn would replace equivalent courses during the academic year. Overstaffing could be reduced by this means.

3. Through an overall evaluation process, the chairman may be able to determine whether or not the student

FTE has dropped due to a lack of competence of faculty. Enrollment decline is sometimes influenced by this factor.

4. Documentation should be available to support department efforts that have addressed the problems. Participating faculty should be noted and commended.

5. Credentials of all faculty members should be reviewed thoroughly to determine existing strengths and weaknesses in *all* teaching areas of the department. This is a critical endeavor, since preparation for retraining or retrenchment may be based on these credentials.

The chairperson should be prepared to point out to the dean that the department is being asked to absorb a 10-percent reduction when the overall reduction to the institution will be only 6 percent. He should also inquire whether student pressure should be allowed to prevent a reasonable increase in fees. Dr. Tongue's specific proposal should include the following points:

1. A plan to decrease the number of hours the language laboratory will be open. This reduction will be based on a usage-demand time line.

2. A plan to decrease the number of part-time lecturers that are now being used.

3. A plan to share some faculty member or members with other departments in which they may be qualified to teach.

4. The assignment of faculty members to teaching a summer session course or courses.

5. An overall plan designed to retrain professors so they are competent in two or three disciplines within the division, particularly Spanish. This should be done through sabbatical leaves and staff-development activities.

6. Any reassignments congruent with qualifications, for example, library, research, grantsmanship.

7. A decrease in department expense through the operating budget.

8. A decrease in or the elimination of all travel.

9. A decrease in *any* expenditures that cannot be justified by faculty.

10. A long-range plan for staff reduction, strictly within the legal guidelines of the university.

(Francis C. Compestine, Chairman, Division of Mathematics, Aims Community College, Greeley, Colorado.)

Response #2

Management of decline appears to be a reality at Eastern University and administrators and faculty, in the words of K. E. Boulding, are being challenged to carry out the "management of decline" with "empathy and . . . an all too rare mixture of compassion and realism" and develop a "creative widening of agendas."

Several questions emerge. Has Eastern been planning for the contingency of decline? What kind of university-wide academic program and fiscal planning exists? Has there been a clear analysis and articulation of institutional goals and priorities as related to the mission of Eastern University? Openness and participation are key ingredients in understanding and supporting retrenchment measures in both academic and administrative areas. However, there does not seem to be a commitment and consensus from faculty, students, and support staff on institutional concerns at Eastern and thus more productive and positive involvement of these constituents in the future of the institution. Have the faculty, students, and support staff been educated to the programmatic and fiscal realities of Eastern University? Has the faculty been included in determining the appropriate strategies for developing resource flexibility, enhancing intellectual vitality, and meeting the rising cost of instruction? These are some questions Dr. Tongue should raise with other department members, students, and the dean when they meet. Tongue should also address the issue of decline in his department.

In cutting department expenses, Tongue may wish to discuss the following four strategies with his colleagues: (1) the limiting of course offerings in each of the foreign language areas, (2) the possibility of program termination of Greek or Latin or both, (3) staffing adjustments, and (4) the consolidation of department activities. Again, questions must be raised. Specifically, which foreign-language programs are *most crucial* to Eastern University's mission? Which foreign language programs are *less central* to the functioning of the department and university? In regard to long-range priorities: What are the long-range priorities of foreign languages in terms of *quality*? What are short-range allocation priorities in terms of dollars, positions, facilities, etc? Only after colleagues have grappled with these issues can personnel decisions be addressed. In order to ensure flexibility in the already "tenured-in" situation, the two assistant professors in Spanish might be terminated and replaced with adjuncts or full-time faculty members from other languages who are qualified to teach Spanish. The part-time lecturers in French and Italian should be terminated. The serious possibility of terminating either Latin or Greek or both must be addressed; this is a ticklish issue, since the Latin professor chairs the department. Do either of these full professors have competencies in other areas? Can they be retrained? Retraining fellowships might be offered to tenured professors in exchange for "voluntary resignation." Faculty in midcareer who are ambitious but frustrated in their academic pursuits as a result of a lack of mobility, declining enrollments, and scarcity of institutional resources might welcome such fellowships and an opportunity to retrain in another profession.

No single strategy may be relied upon by the foreign language department to present proposals for reducing the level of department expense by 10 percent and 20 percent. However, the cumulative effect of the savings from each of the above strategies or a combination of them can be substantial. (Toni Iadarola, Provost, College of Mount St. Joseph on the Ohio, Mount St. Joseph, Ohio.)

Response #3

Dr. Tongue needs to be prepared to discuss his department staffing situation in terms of several different factors: education philosophy, department personnel, and curriculum. He needs to prepare for his meeting with the dean in several ways: by consulting on strategy and tactics with respected and informed members of the department, by gathering and analyzing accurate data on total student credit hours generated, cost per student credit hour, quality of department teaching and research, and other quantitative factors, and by preparing alternative plans of action.

Before the meeting with the dean he ought to discuss frankly and openly the various aspects of the problem with his staff at a faculty meeting. Students and others who press for answers to rumors should be responded to with a frank admission that the institution faces serious problems and will have to take decisive steps to solve them, but the degree to which this will affect the department of foreign languages has yet to be determined.

Upon meeting with the dean, Dr. Tongue should first listen to the dean's concerns and, if some are provided, his suggestions for reducing the department budget. In general, Dr. Tongue should try to avoid suggesting any new targets for a knife-wielding administrator to attack. Throughout the discussion, Dr. Tongue should strive continually to remind the dean that foreign-language teaching is at the core of essential university activities, that in the 1980's, especially in light of the report of the President's Commission on Foreign Language Study, books by Richard Brod of MLA and United States representative Paul Simon, the increasing non-English-speaking population of the United States in general and the local urban area in particular, the unfavorable international-trade balance of the United States, etc., Eastern University must do more than ever to serve its mature and perceptive students by providing increased opportunities for international studies, including foreign languages.

Assuming that the dean smiles with stoic resignation at these strong, cogent philosophical arguments and, knowing that the arts and humanities are always the most vulnerable targets, brushes them aside, saying, "Yes, but about that ten-to-twenty-percent reduction . . . ," Dr. Tongue must then be prepared to negotiate in earnest. His goal must be to retain the two untenured assistant professors of Spanish in order to maintain the viability of his program. He could present three plans of action:

1. Propose releasing the three part-time lecturers in French and Italian. This will not hurt the program in Italian, where enrollments have fallen drastically. Some problem will be created in French, where staffing will be somewhat short.

2. Propose that Dr. Tongue himself (a professor of Latin) and one professor of German, both of whom have studied French extensively in the past, refresh somewhat their French over the summer, making them more than competent to teach an introductory course in that language.

3. Propose the introduction of major curriculum revisions. Courses in Greek and Latin culture and civilization (which will not in any way conflict with or duplicate course offerings in the history department), mythology, and modern Spanish, German, French, and Italian civilizations will be made available. These will be designed as large lecture courses, capable of accommodating up to two hundred students, thus improving the department's average class size considerably, and, at the same time, relieving some of the enrollment pressures about which other departments complain. In fact, the addition of a requirement for one course in a foreign civilization would satisfy the department's long-standing desire to increase the lan-

guage requirement and simultaneously contribute to a desirable redistribution of required coursework.

The combination of staff reductions, teaching reassignments, and curriculum innovation will absolutely convince the dean that it is not necessary to terminate the two assistant professors of Spanish. Furthermore, the dean will be so impressed by Dr. Tongue's excellence as a manager of funds and personnel that he will invite him to fill the recently opened .5 FTE position of associate dean, further alleviating the department staffing problem. (Howard Mancing, Associate Professor of Spanish, University of Missouri/Columbia.)

D. "Part-time Faculty"—For or Against?

A related issue concerns the retention of maximum flexibility for the department. Many would argue that such capability is best achieved and retained only when significant use is made of part-time or adjunct faculty. A department committed to using only full-time faculty is stuck with the competencies they possess; changes can occur only slowly, as individuals develop new interests or leave the department and are replaced. By contrast, use of part-time faculty whose contracts are written on a term-by-term basis permits quick response to change in student interests, community needs, and institutional mission. However, full-time faculty may well resist this practice for reasons reviewed in the following case study.

PART-TIME FACULTY

Dr. Alphonso, the chair of the department of public administration, found himself facing the same, seemingly intractable, staffing problem once again. Blessed with a recent surge in student interest, the department had been experiencing enrollment increases in each of the past five years. Compared with other department chairs, particularly those in biology and history, Alphonso knew that he was in an enviable position. He also knew that they did not appreciate his particular set of problems. For a variety of reasons he had in the past used a large number of part-time instructors. The full-time faculty members were not happy with this arrangement, however, and there had been some heated exchanges.

He had argued that the many advantages of using part-time adjuncts justified the department's reliance on them. To begin with, such an arrangement permitted the department to respond quickly to changes in the field and in student interest. None of the full-time faculty, for instance, had been prepared to offer the course in public health-care financing that had proved so popular last year. Student interest in the course had grown so rapidly that Alphonso felt sure that the college dean would have been visited by a student delegation had the course not been offered.

The regional agency administrator who taught the course did a superb job, moreover, doubtless because she knew so much about the current issues. It had been a perfect match, for her practical credentials were outstanding and she had great interest in some affiliation with the university. True, she did not have a Ph.D., but she certainly was an authority. In addition, Alphonso hoped, she could well prove useful in placing some of the department's graduates. Since she had a hand in their education, she not only knew several students but would have a natural investment in an enhanced department placement record. And what regular faculty member had her range of contacts? Alphonso suspected the faculty was a little jealous of her career success.

In addition to the clear curricular advantages of using part-time people from the surrounding urban community, there was an enormous financial advantage. At times, in fact, Alphonso felt a little guilty about paying these people only $1,150 for teaching a three-credit course. It was all that the university permitted, however, and obviously it was enough from the market standpoint. If it was exploitation, the part-time people willingly accepted it. Clearly they had their own careers, which they were advancing by university affiliation. Some, he knew, treasured the status they gained in referring to their teaching in conversation with colleagues. Others found that teaching advanced their careers. Still others seemed to do it just for pleasure.

It was the financial dimension, he felt, that was really

bothering the full-time faculty. For any possibility of their teaching overloads for extra pay was jinxed by the availability of the adjuncts. Faculty members in other departments occasionally had such opportunities, he knew, and his own must resent the adjuncts for reducing this possibility. The summer calendar was affected too. By offering courses in the evening during the fall and spring calender—when there seemed to be the greatest demand for them by nontraditional students—the department was reducing the regular demand during the summer. For this very reason, several summer courses the previous year had not met the minimum enrollment criteria. The two department members who had been scheduled to teach them were quite upset.

Alphonso also knew that his full-time faculty members were unhappy with the extra burden of advising and committee work that they had to assume because the part-time faculty was free from these duties. Several times now Alphonso had reviewed at department meetings the finances involved: how full-time faculty members were paid for responsibilities well beyond those of meeting classes. The financial facts were quite clear, but the faculty's resentment still seemed to be strong.

The strongest argument against the use of part-time instructors, he felt, was that they did not contribute to the intellectual critical mass of the department. Because almost all had full-time jobs elsewhere, they were not present for department meetings or casual corridor conversations. They did not conduct ordinary academic research and were not available to chat about the research projects of others. Alphonso had tried to involve them in the regular department colloquiums, but met with little success. Only three in two years had attended the larger college symposiums—and only because they had a formal role to play.

Alphonso was specially concerned about the intellectual level of exchange in the department, but he also felt strongly about the importance of curricular flexibility. There were presently six full-time faculty members and fifteen adjuncts. He knew that he could approach the dean for a seventh full-time position, but that would require surrendering a good portion of the budget for adjuncts. Most of the full-time faculty members were in favor of adding the seventh position, but he felt quite hesitant about doing so. He wondered if he was missing some magic solution to the whole issue.

What steps should Alphonso take in order to develop a clear department policy on the issue—one that enjoys reasonably good acceptance? Remember that any use of part-time or adjunct faculty also generates its own special set of responsibilities for the chairperson. For instance, what procedures should be used for instruction evaluation? How should the full-time faculty be involved in the initial selection and reappointment of adjuncts? What policies should be used for the assignment of desirable courses when both full-time and adjunct faculty members have expressed an interest—especially when the latter have the better credentials?

Response #1

There is no magic solution to the whole issue here. Alphonso's position is unreasonable with the current ratio of six full-time faculty members to fifteen adjuncts. While the potential for full-time faculty dissatisfaction with their work loads relative to the work loads of adjunct faculty always exists, this potential increases with the ratio of adjunct faculty to full-time faculty. The benefits of adjunct faculty for curricular flexibility as perceived by full-time faculty, however, are not likely to increase with an increase in adjunct faculty. If there were considerably fewer adjunct faculty, the dissatisfaction would undoubtably be much less. While Alphonso would indeed sacrifice some flexibility of action with an additional full-time position, given the current ratio there would still be some adjunct faculty to preserve curricular flexibility. Also, the benefits to be gained from an additional full-time faculty member are significant both for the sake of continuity and the full-time faculty's morale.

Alphonso should approach the dean for opening a seventh full-time position after having first discussed quite carefully the disadvantages as well as the advantages of this action with the current full-time faculty. The loss of curricular flexibility and, indeed, budget flexibility should be made clear, and the full-time faculty should be encouraged to find ways to minimize these losses. At the same time, the potential advantages of the remaining adjunct faculty for the department should be stressed. These advantages include not only intellectual interchange among peers, but also the possible professional benefits to full-time faculty of having contacts outside the department through the adjunct faculty—for example, consulting opportunities and research resources. Full-time faculty members should be encouraged to find ways to realize these potential benefits. Through such discussions the full-time faculty would become actively involved in the process of determining how adjunct faculty could best contribute to the department rather than focusing only on the disadvantages associated with them. (Harriet G. Tolpin, Chairperson, Department of Economics, Simmons College, Boston, Massachusetts.)

Response #2

Dr. Alphonso was accustomed to pondering the implications of the division of labor between full-time and part-time faculty. The question of the intellectual critical mass had been a source of concern for him as he reflected on the contributions provided by a *full-time* faculty and fresh reflections on old problems provided by a *new* faculty member. Ironically, this seemingly intractable problem may present him with an opportunity to make a contribution to both areas of concern. He should discuss with the personnel office the possibility of employing a full-time temporary appointment, commonly used to replace an individual on sabbatical leave. He will probably discover that appointments of this type are, by definition, limited to one year in duration but include all responsibilities of a full-time faculty member, with pay that is commensurate with full-time responsibilities.

While this pay rate will diminish his department's ability to offer courses, Alphonso should feel better about the fairness of the salary. Alphonso should utilize this category of employment to fill the authorized vacancies and justify his recommendation to the dean and faculty on the following grounds:

1. The department flexibility would in large part be maintained, since the appointments would be for only one year. This form of appointment would allow for rotation of experts in the program area.

2. This one-year appointment could be of value to many individuals in their career plans, either as a part of a growth program, or as sabbatical leave from their public-administration work, or as a normal part of their career steps from one professional position to another.

3. The one-year appointment would carry with it all full-time responsibilities, including advising and committee work.

4. The new faculty member would be a fresh and professional contributor to the intellectual critical mass of the department.

5. The university could demonstrate an interest in maintaining current programs by offering a one-year appointment to the professionals in the field.

In addition to this basic set of arguments for the full-time temporary appointment, two other benefits could emerge from his proposal. The department of public administration would be identified as an innovator in resolving a problem that had emerged time after time within the academic community. The additional benefit would come in the response from the professional community. Federal, state, and municipal agencies would be inspired by the concept of retraining some of their best professionals in this new program. (Jim Raughton,

Division Director, Science and Technology Division, Community College of Denver, Denver, Colorado.)

E. "The Issue of Fellowships"—Making Do with Less

The current and prospective financial pressures on institutions are making not only for program reduction and redirection, faculty and staff reduction, and debates about the use of adjunct faculty. The financial pressures show up in the other ways too, such as deferred plant maintenance and equipment purchases. Institutionally funded scholarship aid is yet another area in which these pressures find expression. The following case study illustrates some of the difficulties.

THE ISSUE OF FELLOWSHIPS

The financial crunch everyone had been reading about was beginning to show up on campus. The halls were definitely dimmer and dirtier, as utilities and maintenance had been cut back. The grounds seemed shabbier, and the hours of the library had been reduced. However, the measures seemed appropriate responses to an inevitable decline in resources and so were taken without causing complaint or even much comment.

The reduction in fellowships, however, was another matter. For a number of years the English department had been allotted twelve institutionally funded, graduate-level fellowships. The department faculty had found the fellowships to be important recruiting devices, for they were able to attract excellent graduate students who simply would not have come on the reputation of the university alone.

The department had evolved a pattern of distributing the fellowships according to disciplinary areas in which the department had considerable strength. Accordingly, the areas of Elizabethan, Restoration, Victorian, and modern American literatures had each become accustomed to having three full-tuition scholarships. The financial-aid arrangement also included a stipend of $100 a month for living expenses.

The custom had also been to support students for three years. By the end of that time the students were usually finished wih coursework. Some had even been able to find teaching jobs on the strength of the work they had already done toward the dissertation. Of course, that had not happened recently. At any rate, the fellowships were advertised and awarded on the basis of merit, and the department was accustomed to making four new awards each year. Traditionally each of the prominent discipline areas laid claim to one of the slots, though occasionally there had been adjustments.

Suddenly, however, this comfortable tradition was to be broken. The department had learned just a week earlier from the central administration that funds would simply not be provided the next year for four of the fellowships. Funds for only eight would be available. The English department was not being singled out, as all academic areas had been reduced.

As Dorian, chairperson of the department, reflected on the matter, it appeared that the department needed to make several decisions. One issue was the amount that should go for recruiting as opposed to continuing support. For instance, the funds could be split between years—providing a full first-year support, for instance, with no follow-up. Students presently in their first and second years would then have their support reduced, and decisions would have to be made on the criteria to be used in determining the reductions. Another possibility was to revise the distribution of the money. This could mean providing two half-year fellowships, for instance, rather than a full one. On the other hand, the department might then lose the top students it needed. Perhaps the department should simply abandon the principle of merit and distribute the available money on the basis of financial need.

The more Dorian thought about the matter, the more issues there seemed to be. Could the department count on the university to restore the previous level of scholarship funding? Was this the time to reduce the range of goals the department was trying to accomplish?

How would you advise Dorian on the way to proceed? What are the appropriate solutions?

This is not a happy situation and future prospects are not clear. Consider the following responses.

Response #1

The cutbacks clearly have the potential for a reduction, perhaps even collapse, of the quality and size of the graduate program. In addition, the cutbacks and their inherent ramifications have the potential for interfaculty and interscholarship area wrangling and unhappiness. The chairman needs to move swiftly to alleviate or minimize the potential negative effects on the graduate program and to prevent faculty dissention.

The situation presented to Dorian emphasized rather clearly the constant need for chairpersons addressing problems to remember their role as middle-managers. In order to fully deal with this situation, Dorian needs to pursue the matter with the administration, with fellow chairpersons, and with the department.

Dorian should pursue the matter with the administration for two important reasons. First, by sharing his concerns about the situation with higher administrators he will register with them the specific negative ramifications of the cutbacks. As a consequence there may be more reluctance to make any further cutbacks at a later date, or at least provide more appropriate consultation than has occurred this time. A failure to share these concerns with the administration may well give them the wrong signal and open up the prospect for a repetition of the cutbacks. Second, Dorian must be able to demonstrate to his faculty that he has not simply acquiesced on the matter.

Dorian needs to pursue the matter with his fellow chairpersons. Since the cutbacks were made across the board, Dorian's overtures on his own to the administration for a repeal of the cutbacks would be unlikely to be accommodated. On the other hand, a firm front from the collective chairpersons might be able to achieve a reduction, in part or in whole, in the cutbacks. At the very least, such collective action would make a firm impression on the administrators and might avert any similar future cutbacks being promulgated by routine fiat. Again, any actions taken along these lines would emphasize to Dorian's faculty that he was pursuing the matter on a number of fronts.

Dorian, obviously, must also pursue the matter within the department. In this regard he needs to achieve a short-term and a long-term solution. Obviously there is an immediate problem for the imminent award of the fellowships for the next year. He must take care to prevent tensions arising between faculty and between scholarship areas at this point. His central goal therefore should be: (1) to assure the faculty that he is pursuing the repeal or reduction of the cutbacks with the administration, (2) to achieve a completely equal arrangement between scholarship areas for the next year's awards (for instance, a proposal could be made that each scholarship area receive two fellowships and that the decision and award of these fellowships be left to the area's faculty), (3) to propose a task force to review the long-term ramifications of the cutbacks, if maintained, and to report back with recommendations to the faculty on a strategic plan for the department to deal with these cutbacks in the long term in event that they are to be continued. (Robert P. Lowndes, Professor and Chairman, Department of Physics, Northeastern University, Boston, Massachussetts.)

Response #2

Dorian should boldly face the possibility of reducing the scope of his graduate program. In difficult times, responsible and sensitive faculty members will accept sacrifices that are required by financial realities but that may ultimately benefit the department and the profession.

The number of fellowships offered should be reduced and new awards should be made on the basis of merit. As the continuation of support is an essential incentive to good students, the level of support should remain constant and should be continued for three years to students whose work meets the department's expectations. The number of graduate students in the department will probably decrease with the number of fellowships offered, but quality will be maintained and perhaps even improved as only the truly outstanding students will be supported. An eventual reduction in the total number of Ph.D.s awarded is a healthy contribution to the employment situation in the profession, especially when there is some assurance that those encouraged to attend graduate school are outstanding candidates.

The department should be careful not to lower its entrance standards to make up for the potential loss of students caused by the decreased available support.

The loss of four fellowships in the first year creates a serious recruitment problem. Presumably eight graduate students will expect to continue with fellowship support that will leave nothing for new students. Armed with a specific plan for and response to a reduction in the number of graduate students, Dorian should confront his dean, expressing his reluctant agreement to retrench over two years but maintaining his need for at least ten fellowships for the coming year. A reasonable dean will try to satisfy Dorian's request, especially if Dorian indicates that his department is willing to make sacrifices. At a last resort, Dorian could ask the eight continuing graduate students if they would be willing to accept a 12.5 percent reduction in their fellowships for one year in order to provide one additional fellowship for a new student. (Paul J. Schwartz, Chairman, Department of Modern and Classical Languages, University of North Dakota, Grand Forks, North Dakota.)

In other ways, too, chairpersons must deal with the issue of department productivity. More often than not, this requires introducing change. But change does not come easily for faculty members. In fact, they are notorious for resisting changes in the way things are done as well as in the things to be done. It may be that this common conservativeness of faculty members is a function of their basic professional responsibility to be guardians and transmitters of knowledge.

In any case, it is the chairperson who has to monitor, and frequently to initiate, department change. There are fewer carrots or sticks available now with which to motivate faculty. External and internal review processes provide important road maps, but fiscal realities allow little money to reward merit, and unless untenured the unproductive faculty member is not easy to release. Personal persuasion and persuasiveness remain the key tools for the chairperson.

—————— CHAPTER SIX ——————

Other Problems and Special Circumstances

To THE CASUAL OBSERVER, a list of the various responsibilities of the department chairperson must read much like a long laundry list. Specific, identifiable tasks can easily number in the fifties, and the sheer range of activities can numb the mind. One must distinguish among their importance, of course, and each chairperson must make ongoing decisions as to priority and urgency. We have already looked at a number of these tasks. This chapter focuses on several other issues that chairpersons may have to confront and that can have a certain immediacy.

For various reasons our times show an increased awareness of the ethical dimensions to both corporate and individual behavior. The whole cluster of acts that we know as Watergate reminds us of ethical difficulties in government. Questionable payments abroad have raised moral concerns about business practices. Colleges and universities are not immune to scrutiny. The various scandals connected with athletics have demonstrated that.

Indeed, higher education is rich in areas of potential moral abuse. Throughout there is a special trust at stake—a responsibility both to learning and to the student. Professionals in higher education are certainly presented with a variety of opportunities—and temptations—to exploit the special relationships common in organized learning for personal pleasure or profit. As a result, chairpersons will recognize that some of the issues that they face are inextricably moral as well as practical.

A. "The Letter of Recommendation"— Professional and Personal Loyalties

"The Letter of Recommendation" draws our attention to some of these ethical issues and reminds us of the importance of enforcing strict standards of professional behavior at the same time that it suggests how difficult some decisions can be in the process. Specifically, the case study illustrates the problem of faculty-student sexual relationships while also emphasizing some dilemmas involved in supportive colleague attitudes.

THE LETTER OF RECOMMENDATION

Roberta Ritewell had just started looking through the mail. It contained the usual third-class items describing the new publications that her department needed desperately, she was told. She also read a couple of the unsolicited applications that came regularly for nonexistent positions. These she always found depressing. They contained uniformly superb credentials of people she knew had little chance of finding an academic job in today's faculty market. It was troubling because the credentials were frequently better than any that her department could boast of.

What caught her attention, however, was a request for an evaluation of Paul Merrill. Her institution had tried to hush

up the incident involving him, but people still talked occasionally about it. With his new wife, Merrill had come to the
college three years earlier as an extraordinarily promising assistant professor of philosophy. His credentials were excellent, and he had already published a monograph on
Spinoza. He was young, attractive, and full of vigor and enthusiasm. Students flocked to his classes, for he had instantly
gained a reputation as a superb teacher. Ritewell herself
visited his classroom several times and found his reputation
well deserved.

In fact, she took considerable pleasure in having hired
him. The contributions he had made to the department were
impressive. Although there were five other full-time faculty
members in the department, it was Merrill who had really
reversed the decline in student enrollment. Prior to his coming, the department had been regarded a place of serious, but
slightly dull, inquiry. Students took philosophy courses
primarily because of distribution requirements, and there had
been few majors or minors. Within a semester after his arrival
the situation turned around, and philosophy was being talked
about as a significant and interesting discipline. Enrollment
turned up, and the number of people seeking departmental
minors started to jump.

There was absolutely no doubt that Merrill was a first-rate
instructor. The student evaluations were uniformly high, even
in the required logic class. He was conscientious about his
committee assignments, was always available for student advising, and still was able to do some research and writing. In
fact, he had produced what Ritewell regarded as a first-class
article on the latent solipsism of Gilbert Ryle.

The scandal broke when one of his sophomore students
went to the college dean with the news that she was pregnant
by Merrill. Student pregnancies had been heard of before, of
course, but never had the student been the daughter of the
president of the local conservative club. The club was an organization of important community leaders, most of whom
regarded the college with some suspicion as a hothouse of
radicalism. Despite the hostility, members of the club were in
a position to exercise considerable influence upon the college
administration, and apparently they did in this case.

Within three days after Ritewell first heard of the scandal,

Merrill came by to say that he had just been advised by the president that his teaching responsibilities at the college would end with final exams, in three weeks, and that his contract for the next year would be revoked. Ritewell was upset that she had not been involved in this decision and told Merrill that she was prepared to stand by him to secure due process in the matter.

He declined the offer, though, indicating that he preferred simply to leave without fanfare. His involvement with the student had been a mistake, he knew, and he could see no good coming from contesting dismissal. While he was not innocent of the charge, he had been vulnerable to the student's attentions because of problems he and his wife were having. Curiously, it now seemed that the affair could restore the relationship. He wanted that to happen, and he was prepared to leave quietly. He wanted only Ritewell's assurance that she would stand by him in the future with appropriate letters of reference. While Ritewell certainly did not approve of intimacies with students, she was quite impressed by Merrill's contributions to the department and so readily agreed to his request.

Now, however, Ritewell was not sure how she should respond to the letter. For one thing, after Merrill left, a rather strong rumor circulated that he had been involved with other students as well. Ritewell was not one to be governed by rumors, but she also felt that there was an ethics to the profession and that it cut against the behavior in which Merrill had at least once engaged. On the other hand, students were more practiced today, at least (and perhaps only) in respect to sexual behavior, and who was she to comment on what faculty did outside the classroom?

Looking again at the letter, she noticed that it was from a small, religiously affiliated college that had only recently gone co-ed. She wanted very much to support Merrill, for he was, after all, an excellent teacher. She knew she had an obligation to him as well as one to the profession. As a consequence, she was unsure how much information she should supply in her response. What should she say?

How different would your response be if Merrill had instead been dismissed for drug-related activity? Assume, for instance, that he had spent much time at student hangouts —one of which was raided by the police when he was there. The police alleged that Merrill had been partaking of illegal drugs. Merrill did not contest the charge, pleading nolo contendere. Other features of the case remain as stated above —the president responds to community pressure to crack down on college drug activity, Merrill's contract for next year is revoked, etc. What should Ritewell say in this case?

General questions that can be explored include: What are one's obligations to other institutions in commenting on colleagues and associates? To what extent should one volunteer unfavorable information? The converse is also involved. What are one's obligations to colleagues—particularly where, as in this case, conditions may have changed since promises were made in a moment of weakness?

Discussion should also deal directly with faculty responsibilities in matters of drug abuse and of sexual involvement with students. How should one evaluate the claim of the faculty member who argues that what he or she does out of the classroom is none of the institution's business? How relevant is the issue of who takes the initiative in such involvements? What, in general, are the requirements of professionalism in our age of liberalized sexual conduct? Consider the following, quite different, responses.

Response #1

Although Merrill's unfortunate relationship with a student could not be condoned, it was, in a sense, understandable. One can imagine that the pressures on a young faculty member to perform, especially at Merrill's level of achievement, might be accompanied by domestic confusion and the need for outside affection and support. Equally inopportune was the student's connection with the conservative club and the fact that the club members were important community leaders. We can assume that Merrill was fired because a public scandal had embarrassed the college administration, not because the president was fanatically opposed to private teacher-student relationships. In a sense, Merrill's real "sin" was that a private matter, one that should probably not have occurred at all, became a public issue and embarrassed the college.

Surely this sort of thing is not likely to happen again to Mr. Merrill. His home life improved, and he has learned where not to go for affection and support. Besides, no one could be so unlucky twice!

Ms. Ritewell should therefore confine her letter of recommendation to describing Merrill's academic achievements and teaching skills. Merrill is not someone who habitually compromises himself and his college, and Ritewell should feel comfortable describing him as a splendid teacher and skilled researcher. Mentioning the "scandal" could severely damage Merrill's chances of employment. The chairperson should be willing to risk some potential personal embarrassment to prevent an isolated incident from ruining a promising career. If necessary, she could defend her recommendation based on Merrill's character and the value of his contributions to the department.

By contrast, the faculty member who frequents student hangouts and uses drugs cannot be defended by the above arguments. His indiscretion is public, not private. He has embarrassed the college not by accident, but through habitual carelessness. His predicament is the result not of an isolated incident, but of his lifestyle. The chairperson's letter in this case should definitely cite the incident, since it is likely to happen again. (David Browder, Chairman, Department of Mathematics, Simmons College, Boston, Massachusetts.)

Response #2

Whether or not Paul Merrill had been an asset to the university's image for his teaching behavior or for being a real "live wire" should be given minor consideration in this matter. The more important issue is that the process used to terminate him is loaded with caveats for the rest of the faculty. While a university president needs to be responsive to the public in general, and especially the organized "publics," he or she must follow due process in a systematic fashion or else key decisions will continue to be executed by administrative fiat—dooming faculty morale.

The students will likely split into three groups: (1) those who will be appalled at Merrill's *alleged* behavior, (2) those who couldn't care less, and (3) those who will raise holy hell because their intellectual savant is being handled as a wayward adolescent by the surrogate parent—the president. Would the university benefit from the students' reactions? Probably not!

The faculty will likely split into: (1) those who will be appalled, (2) those who will cry, *"C'est la vie,"* and (3) those metatypes who will see that due process is being violated and the president's wrath could go astray in the future for some other reason.

Ritewell would be well advised to alert her faculty and her fellow chairs concerning the implications of the president's modus operandi. A council of chairs should be formed to deal with procedural matters involving the due-process issue.

Definite process should be established and implemented *now*, using the Merrill incident as the catalyst. The university should show the public its interest in the latter's inputs, but at the same time the faculty and the administration should also demonstrate more than knee-jerking behavior in matters such as Merrill's or any others of a more or less serious nature.

Her response should be tempered by the notion of the involvement being *alleged*, by the notion that someone is innocent until proven guilty, and by a modicum of tolerance for others' indiscretions. Did Merrill really break a law and could he be guilty of felonious behavior (a criterion usually sufficient to be removed from his job)? Was he set up? The girl, a de facto adult, is not without culpability. Merrill's lack of discretion is something generic that also has to be dealt with by the chairs and faculty. What constitutes the threshold for determining one's behavior being ethical or unethical? Does the university code specify this?

On the more pragmatic side, as a chair, I would stand by Merrill as far as his due process is concerned, but when it comes to recommending him for further employment a contingency system could be enacted. I personally would only recommend him if he could demonstrate that his personal life would no longer interfere with his and others' professional roles. The "conservative" club can't "try" him (only the courts can), but it can certainly bring pressures to bear on him and all those who did not participate in his demise. Again, the faculty must police its own ranks. Ritewell, however, can refuse to recommend him for further employment until he demonstrates he is capable of being recommended. After all, Ritewell can only respond positively to his teaching performance. What is she to do in the other areas of performance: leave these areas *blank*? I personally would request Merrill attend marriage counseling or personal counseling to turn around his preadult excursions if he wanted a letter from me. I would have no interest in passing his "social experimentations" along with his professional excellence. The two are not unrelated, the letter of the law notwithstanding. (Fred E. Kirschner, Chairman, Counseling and Educational Psychology and Foundations, University of Nevada/Las Vegas.)

The chairperson has a fundamental responsibility to support colleagues in the face of undocumented charges. Special difficulties are created when this responsibility comes into conflict with the equally important responsibilities one has to students and to the standards of the profession. For instance, we are seeing increased awareness of the incidence of various forms of sexual harrassment of students by faculty and administrators. Chairpersons should be alert to the need to respond appropriately to claims of such harrassment. In fact, such claims can be ignored only at the risk of later legal sanctions. The important issue here is, how is one to gather relevant evidence? This issue is especially sensitive, for one must at the same time both support faculty members and investigate student complaints.

B.   "The Questionnaire"—Coping with Bad Judgment

Other issues of an intractable moral dimension can also arise. The following case presents several concerns that can stem from the apparent violation of professional ethics by a department faculty member. Among these concerns is the proper allegiance to the department that one ought to be able to expect from faculty members. The chairperson in "The Questionnaire" must also deal with repairing the resulting damage to the department and to the university. In addition, the chairperson must reflect on what would be an appropriate institutional response to the individual's behavior.

THE QUESTIONNAIRE

The damage was already done, Joan knew. The issue now was how to put the best face on it and what to do about its prime cause. The recent events had certainly been upsetting. The incident was just the sort of thing that the sociology department did not need, for the publicity tended to reinforce an image of both eccentricity and unprofessionalism.

It was all the fault of Jim Nelson and his questionnaire. Some were now charging him with prurient interests simply because of his questionnaire on the sexual practices of middle-aged white-collar males. But the information that could be gained in this way might be of genuine scholarly interest. It was rather the way he had conducted the actual scholarly inquiry that really ignited things.

One of the community leaders to whom the instrument had been sent had in an idle moment removed the staple joining the pages and noticed the tiny numbers written there. His suspicions aroused, the man informed the university president of his concern. As luck would have it, the individual was prominent within the community and important to the university. As a result, Joan received a call from the president that very day.

Immediately afterward she went to Nelson's office. Upon hearing from her of the president's concern, Nelson indicated that in fact the questionnaire had been secretly coded. It was all done in the name of increased knowledge, he had said. It would be quite instructive to correlate some of the responses with types of management position. That was not the sort of information he could expect people to reveal voluntarily, however, and so this stratagem had been devised to secure it. There was no other way he knew of to obtain the data. While he had indeed promised the respondents complete anonymity in the covering letter, he was confident of his ability to utilize this secret information in a fashion that would protect individual identities.

Besides, Nelson had added, it was his own private research project and had no official connection with the university. He had used his own personal funds for both duplication of the materials and for postage. Department stationery had not been used for the cover letter. True, he had identified himself there as a member of the sociology department, but that was simply to give credibility to the project.

His advice to her, he continued, was simply to stall. People would soon forget and the present furor would disappear. The present issue was one of bad luck and nothing else. If the staple had not been removed there would be no controversy. In any event, he was a tenured member of the faculty and he deeply resented this questioning of his judgment and of his ability to keep professional confidences. If she persisted in pestering him, he would not be adverse to filing a grievance.

Reflecting afterward on the conversation, Joan wondered what her next step should be. In her judgment it was clear that Nelson had violated a fundamental ethical principle of the profession. He was not the first to do so, however, and much previous knowledge had been gained in this manner. In any case, how should she answer his claim that the project was a personal undertaking and unconnected with the department or university?

At that point in her reflections the telephone rang and a reporter from the city newspaper asked for her perspective on the events and what action against Nelson she as department chairperson might be contemplating.

How should Joan respond to the reporter? What should she do about Jim?

The basic facts seem not to be an issue here. At least Jim Nelson has acknowledged that the survey instruments were secretly coded, despite his contrary assurances to the recipients. Nelson evidences no obvious concern for the department or university, however, and indicates a clear pugnaciousness about future discussions of the issue. Certainly he seems to have few scruples about the niceties of professional standards. Clearly he presents a potential for future conflict. What should the chairperson do next? How can she generate within him a greater appreciation for, or loyalty to, the department itself? How, if at all, can she forestall similar incidents in the future? In very different ways, the following responses touch on some of these issues.

Response #1

Joan's only realistic choice is to inform the reporter that she regrets the incident but that she must talk further with the president and that any statement would probably come from his office.

Nelson is clearly in the wrong. He violated a trust after informing the respondents they would have complete anonymity. His duplicity in the matter makes his threat to file a grievance if Joan persisted in questioning him pure bluff. Though he did not use department stationery, he did clearly identify himself as a member of the faculty, and so the fact that he was engaged in a private research project is beside the point. The integrity of the university is therefore in question, and Nelson should be so told, either directly by the president or by the chairperson after consultation with the president.

Harmony between town and gown can be restored only if the university states it cannot condone such practice by a member of its faculty. (Robert L. Reid, Chairman, Department of History, Baylor University, Waco, Texas.)

Response #2

Professor Nelson crossed the line from poor judgment to blatantly unethical behavior when he secretly coded his questionnaires. As the research subjects were informed that their responses would be anonymous, Jim both violated their confidentiality and voided their consent to participate. In practical terms he could easily have foreseen the possibility that the coding would have been discovered. This is a serious offense that cannot be justified by the knowledge to be gained. When Jim identified himself as a member of the department of sociology he involved the university.

Still, the chairperson simply cannot be responsible for the breach of professional ethics in outside pursuits by individual department members. She should stay as uninvolved as possible with this problem. As a first step, this means to stay *completely* unavailable to the press for comments on the situation. It is important for her to realize that any public statements of censure are potentially defamatory.

Within the institution there should be a procedure for handling this type of problem. The chairperson should check with the dean or academic vice-president to find out what it is. Many institutions have a human subjects review board or a research committee. It may be wise for the chairperson also to seek advice from the university's legal counsel about how she should proceed and what records should be kept.

I believe the chairperson should keep as low a profile as possible and avoid saying or doing anything that could involve the department in this matter. She should advise other department members to do likewise. This is not a problem to be tackled at the department level. (Elizabeth V. Swenson, Associate Professor and Chairperson, Department of Psychology, John Carroll University, Cleveland, Ohio.)

C. "The Handicapped Student"— Changing Practices and Attitudes

The moral sensitivities of our age have created new issues and challenges. It is not simply the obvious acts of unprofessional conduct or of social injustice that the chairperson may have to handle. Other personally sensitive issues can arise with regard to which the chairperson has to exercise leadership. Sometimes special creative efforts are called for. Consider the challenge presented in the following case study, dealing with accommodating the handicapped student.

THE HANDICAPPED STUDENT

The problem was an unusually challenging one. Although Tim had been chairperson for three years, he could not immediately see any obvious solutions. But something had to be done. Two students had already visited his office to indicate the difficulty they were experiencing. The faculty member involved had also stopped by to discuss the discomfort he was feeling.

The student who was the immediate cause of all of this was Bob Winters, a victim of cerebral palsy. Confined to a wheelchair, Winters was an extraordinarily determined individual, committed to participating fully in his classes, completing his degree, and pursuing a career in elementary education. One could only have admiration, Tim thought, for Bob's determination to surmount adversity. For the obstacles to Bob's goals were not simply in his own body, significant though these were. It was the reaction of others that frequently compounded his problems.

At any rate, that seemed to be happening here. What had in earlier semesters been an exciting and stimulating course, one with a reputation as a "must" for majors in the department, was now a problem course. And the reason was the response of the other students to Winters' condition. The class

enrollment was deliberately kept low in order to allow for a
fairly intense level of student discussion. But with only ten
students in class, the difficulties Winters had in speaking and
in being understood were all too obvious.

Other students were clearly troubled by him. Despite
themselves, they were repulsed by Winters' appearance and
exasperated by the difficulty in understanding his comments.
Not only was his speech slurred, it seemed to take forever in
coming. Still, he persisted in trying to contribute to the class.
As a result, the zing had completely disappeared from the
class sessions. Attendance was falling off as well—in fact,
Winters was the only one with a perfect attendance record.

Julian Cohen, the faculty member involved, had indicated
his own distress at the turn matters had taken. On the one
hand, he commented to Tim, this was his favorite course and
the only one in the current semester that he really enjoyed. He
felt some understandable scholarly disappointment that
things were working out so poorly. In fact, he had hoped to
share with the class some writing he was doing in order to
profit from their responses. That seemed to be out of the question now, though, since the class progress was so slow. They
would be lucky to get through the minimal amount of material.

On the other hand, Cohen continued, he was troubled that
he had these feelings of resentment. Winters deserved the
absolute best that he could provide, and they all could learn
from him. And not just about determination either, though
that was enormously important, for Winters was quite capable
intellectually. The problem was how to create the conditions
that would make that possible.

Something had to be done soon, Tim knew, for the two
students who had come by earlier had indicated they were
thinking about dropping the course. What options should
Tim explore? How, within the department, can he create
greater sensitivity toward, and acceptance of, handicapped
students? What, if any, special responsibilities does the faculty have toward them?

Institutions are increasingly becoming sensitive to the
special circumstances of the handicapped and other minori-

ties. Problems remain in implementing good intentions, however. Attitudes are difficult to change, and adjustments may need to be made in teaching styles and techniques. Should there also be adjustments in the institution's *expectations* of student performance?

Consider the following responses.

Response #1

This is an especially difficult and delicate case. We might view it in ethical terms: how can we further the common good without overriding the rights of any one individual? The overall goal of the class is clearly in jeopardy here, but, just as clearly, Winters has the right to be in the course.

I would suggest that Cohen begin by talking frankly with Winters about the problem. Chances are good that Winters had experience with how to relieve such tensions. Perhaps he could meet independently with Cohen before each session, and Cohen could relay some of Winters' comments to the class.

Next I would suggest that Cohen, Winters, and the entire class spend some time talking honestly about their feelings and suggesting ways of facilitating class meetings. I recognize how difficult and potentially embarrassing this might prove but, frankly, to proceed without discussing the issue openly seems unbearable.

Finally, I suggest that Cohen offer to make himself available for a reasonable amount of time each week (say, an hour) to work one-on-one with Winters. This could help to minimize the amount of time that Winters needs to speak in class. (George L. Goodwin, Chair, Theology Department, The College of Saint Catherine, St. Paul, Minnesota.)

Response #2

The presence of a handicapped student, such as the one described in this vignette, only serves to bring into focus two preexisting problems: the rigidity of the instructor and the intolerance of the students.

Professor Cohen has chosen to teach his course in the same old way despite the fact that the class enrollees this particular semester make his method ineffective. Federal regulations mandate that course requirements be accommodated to the capabilities of the handicapped student. For a group with this composition, there is entirely too much emphasis on class discussion.

Fortunately, Cohen has recognized that a problem exists and has sought out the advice of the chairman. Tim can and should encourage the instructor to consider taking a more active role in lecturing to the class, having the necessary discussion take place in small subgroups so that class members could take turns interacting with the handicapped student, or requiring that student ideas be written and presented as papers to the class. Perhaps, in addition, the professor has unassertively allowed Winters to monopolize class discussion time, being unsure and uncomfortable about not permitting him to say everything that he wants to. Class discussions need to be controlled in scope and length by the professor. He should not let Winters' difficulty in communication intimidate him.

Students' expressions of repulsion and exasperation urgently need to be dealt with. Students who learn to be tolerant and accepting of another's handicap and to relate to his or her basic human qualities will have learned more from this experience than from anything they could have gained from the course content. It is certainly worthwhile to devote one whole class period, or a block of time outside of class, if available, to a discussion of this problem with an experienced group facilitator.

The chairman owes a legal duty to Winters to accommodate the course requirements to his handicap, and a moral duty to the students in the department to make them aware that first Winters is human and only second is he handicapped. (Elizabeth V. Swenson, Associate Professor and Chairperson,

Department of Psychology, John Carroll University, Cleveland, Ohio.)

Both respondents rightly point out the necessity for adjustments in instruction techniques as well as attitudes when handicapped individuals are involved. Swenson's point about making *appropriate* allowances is an important one, for too often the wrong kind of adjustments are made. It is the manner of conducting discussion time that needs adjustment here, not extending the class time allotted to one individual. Incidentally, many colleges and universities have special resource specialists who can provide assistance to departments in exploring appropriate changes. These individuals may also be skilled in conducting the kind of class discussion about feelings and attitudes that both respondents call for.

D. "Problems with the Dean"— A Question of Strategy

Never far from the chairperson's mind must be the academic or college dean. Both colleague and supervisor, the dean stands in the same uneasy relationship to the chairperson as the latter does to department faculty members. In the best of circumstances, there can be elements of concern and apprehension in the minds of the chairpersons about their deans. Special problems are clearly created, therefore, when the dean exercises poor leadership or in other ways fails to support the chairperson. Consider the following case.

PROBLEMS WITH THE DEAN

The dean was a weak and vindictive individual. So it appeared to Carla Mae Rittehouse and other department chairpersons. Certainly he was a sharp thorn in their sides.

To begin with, he made a great show of his belief in complete openness and participatory democracy. Everything was to be public, he had stated many times, and nothing was to be secret. In reality, however, just about the complete opposite was the case. For one thing, information was rarely shared and chairpersons found out new policies only at the last minute. If they learned of them earlier it was usually by sheer accident. Rarely did they have an opportunity to contribute to the formation of new policies. And when they were consulted there was often little evidence later that they had been heard.

Such inconsistencies between speech and behavior were difficult to put up with. In addition, however, the dean had several times displayed a real pettiness of spirit that hardly made one feel appreciated. The first example of this in Carla Mae's experience had been his questioning of her annual leave report. It was the way he took for granted that she had made an error on or actually falsified her statement that had been so troubling. Rather than asking if she were taking some time in compensation for the all-out effort she had made in order to get the accreditation reports submitted on time, an effort involving two weekends and ten very late nights, his questioning put her on the defensive from the outset. Hardly a management technique designed to foster warm relationships, she felt. Other chairs had similar experiences, some of them involving vouchers for obviously legitimate business expenses that had been scrutinized beyond necessity.

However, the real challenge to the department chairpersons turned around what they saw as the dean's penchant for dividing them from their faculty members.

For instance, he seemed not only to tolerate but actually to encourage unhappy faculty members to bypass their department chairs and come directly to him with their grievances. The first time this happened with a member of her faculty, Carla Mae was upset but thought it merely a quirk. The second time she went to the dean, explaining to him that his behavior undermined her authority. The dean seemed surprised by her visit and her complaint and dismissed her concern. "I have an open-door policy," he had said, "and I can hardly tell people not to come in."

The major blow had come the week before, when he overturned her recommendation against tenure for Gloria Nice. It had taken some courage for Carla Mae to do what she thought was the morally correct thing. Gloria was certainly an adequate teacher, but the times now required that one's credentials be more than adequate. Carla Mae knew that it was unfair to individuals who a decade ago would have had no difficulty securing tenured posts, but she felt that one had a greater responsibility to the institution. One should extend university commitments to only the best faculty that could be found.

The dean's position supporting tenure pointed to a curious reversal of their roles, Carla Mae reflected. It was she who should be supporting the members of the department and he who should be taking the broader institutional perspective. In the year that she had been there she had talked about the general situation with other chairpersons in the college several times. They all seemed to have similar feelings about the dean's poor leadership.

No one seemed to have any good ideas about what to do, however. The dean had only been there a year and a half, and the other senior adminstrators appeared to want to wait and give him a chance. At least that was what the other chairpersons were saying. Carla Mae herself had no idea what the other administrators really thought. She did know, however, that the dean was the one who had hired her and would be the one to evaluate her and to determine her salary.

What resources are available to Carla Mae in this situation? What strategies should she consider?

The college or school dean plays such an important role in the fortunes of the chairperson that Carla Mae's concern is understandable. Consider the following responses.

Response #1

There are three steps Carla Mae can take to handle her problem with the dean. First she should define the problem and her goals regarding the problem. Then she should evaluate the resources available to her. Finally, she can outline and follow an action plan.

Defining the problem in a specific but creative way is the most difficult step in problem solving. Carla Mae might define the problem in several different ways. Each of those definitions has implications for her actions. For example, if she sets as her goal, "This miserable dean must go," her action plan might involve circulating a dismissal petition to the other department chairmen and presenting the signed petition to the senior administrators. If her goal is to make the institution run in spite of the dean, she might organize the department chairs and establish committees for promotion, schedule planning, etc. If her goal is help the dean develop some better management skills, she might suggest a feedback session about the current problems.

Let's imagine that Carla Mae prioritizes the possible goals and problem definitions and begins with the optimistic one: that the dean and the department chairs can learn some management skills. Carla Mae needs to assess the resources available to her. She might ask herself these questions:

- Is the dean committed to "openness," to listening to feedback? If so, who will present the feedback—Carla Mae, the chairs, or the senior administrators?

- Does the dean have a confidante who could speak to him? One of the other administrators? His secretary? An older faculty member?

- Are there any existing institutional structures where it would be appropriate to present the issue? Is there a faculty senate or a university ombudsman? Do the chairs meet regularly with the dean? If not, why not?

- Is Carla Mae the best person to organize this? Does she have the political savvy and interpersonal skills to handle the confrontation skillfully?

- Who is responsible for policy making and implementations: a long-range planning committee, senior administrators or trustees?

The answers to the above questions will help Carla Mae to figure out an action plan.

To illustrate how Carla Mae can use her information to plan, let's imagine Carla Mae is a psychology department chair who is extremely skilled in communication skills but recognizes that an older, wiser chair can add credibility to her action plan. She approaches Dr. Owl for some preliminary discussion. They share some perceptions about the dean's lack of skill. They are fairly sure that other chairs are thinking similarly. She approaches the dean to let him know that she and Dr. Owl are beginning a department chairs' support group. The chairs meet over wine and cheese Fridays at 4:00 to discuss common problems and solutions. Carla Mae is careful to steer the discussion away from gripes and toward solutions. At first the dean declines the invitation to sit in, but after the first meeting the chairs make several excellent suggestions to the registrar as a result of their uncovering some schedule conflicts. One chair hears of an ACE workshop for department chairs and deans and suggests that the institution support attendance fees for several people. The dean and several chairs including Carla Mae attend.

While at the ACE meeting, the dean shares some of his relief at the new direction the chairs have taken. He confesses to feeling burdened by all the responsibility the chairs should have been handling and to feeling too overwhelmed to know how to get all chairs to do more. Carla Mae uses this opportunity to skillfully suggest that the chairs need more information to make their decisions and support from the dean to carry out department policy. Relaxed by a martini, he listens eagerly to the department chair's side, pressing her for more details. She keeps in mind that the most helpful feedback is stated positively and specifically. Instead of complaining about the dean's seeming double cross on the Gloria Nice promotion, she requests that he and she work together on department matters that affect the college. He smiles at the notion of a cooperative working relationship and laments, "It's lonely at the top." Dr. Owl joins their conversation, praising the conference and wishing it had come ten years earlier for him. The three of them agree that most academics are not educated for management and could benefit from training workshops before becoming deans and department chairs.

Carla Mae has accomplished much by following a few simple principles:

1. She specified her goals and thought through the implication of each.

2. She built on her strengths—i.e., good interpersonal skills, group skills, the advice of Dr. Owl.

3. She started with the most promising and least risky goal.

4. She used politics, but in a straightforward manner, keeping the dean posted on the department chairs' activities.

5. She stayed open in her own perceptions and admitted the new data of the dean's side of the problem and his willingness to change.

(Susan M. Robison, Associate Professor, Psychology Department, College of Notre Dame of Maryland, Baltimore, Maryland.)

Response #2

Carla Mae is in one of the most difficult situations a chairperson can be. She has two choices. The first choice (the negative one) is simply to resign as chairperson and mumble something about needing more time for scholarly pursuits; the second choice (the positive one) is to respond to the challenges created by a weak and vindictive dean.

Since Carla Mae is not alone in her estimate of the problems, she and other chairpersons having similar difficulties should use the dean's "open-door" policy to request a meeting with him and acquaint him with a frank appraisal of what they see as disturbing elements in maintaining high morale among chairpersons. If he vacillates, which will probably be the case, the group should then tell him they feel the problems are serious enough to take to the upper echelons of the university administration (which also has an open-door policy), where hopefully a resolution of the difficulties can be achieved.

In regard to the dean's overturning Carla Mae's recommendation against tenure for Gloria Nice, Carla Mae should explain to Gloria specific reasons for the decision and then explain clearly to the dean that a most awkward situation has come about in the department and that she would appreciate an item-by-item response in writing from the dean to her (Carla Mae's) reasons for not recommending tenure. She should inform the dean that she feels this is necessary since the members of the department, both tenured and tenure-track, could then be in a better position to judge her position vis-à-vis that of the dean. If the dean refuses to do this, Carla Mae should send a copy of the request she made to the dean, along with her reasons for not recommending tenure, to the chief executive officer of the university.

Such tactics on the part of Carla Mae, and support from other chairpersons concerning related matters, should move the university administration to decide that a mistake was made in filling the position of dean with the present incumbent and that a year and a half has been long enough to ascertain the fact. (Robert L. Reid, Chairman, Department of History, Baylor University, Waco, Texas.)

Fortunately, probably few chairpersons have relationships quite this challenging to cope with. The case does provoke a question about the ultimate strategy, however. At what point, and in what contexts, ought one to consider resignation? Certainly it ought not to be used as a threat unless one is willing to be taken literally. And its impact falls off quickly after the first time it is mentioned.

Other difficulties frequently arise in relationships between the dean and the chairperson. Consider, for instance, the dean who is a perennial optimist, he or she who is forever "cautiously optimistic." One has to admire the determination of this individual to dwell on the positive and to forge ahead despite obstacles that would immobilize others. The disadvantage for the chairperson is getting the dean's attention on issues while they can still be resolved. The advantages of sheer tenacity and of persistence must be considered and weighed against the risk of creating the deaf ear.

In any case, all chairs need to assemble as much data as possible in support of their departmental accomplishments and objectives, and to provide the key points to their deans. Apart from such information, deans are hardly in a position to support departmental requests, particularly when there are higher-level inquiries. Additionally, clear understandings should be sought with the dean on such matters as budget submissions.

E. "The Department Secretary"— Problems of Territoriality and Status

Chairpersons have responsibilities beyond leading their faculty members, dealing with students, handling moral issues, and confronting the dean. Supervising and evaluating the support staff is certainly an additional important responsibility. The department secretary is frequently a crucial figure. The following case study describes one set of circumstances that the chairperson might have to handle.

THE DEPARTMENT SECRETARY

The first time he was really aware of it was when she burst into tears in his office on Friday morning, the week before the end of the semester. It was an extraordinary event, absolutely the last thing one would have expected of her. Unmarried and middle-aged, she had been department secretary for longer than anyone could remember. It seemed that she had always been there. Generations upon generations of students must have passed through the college and graduated as majors under her direction.

She was a veritable living, breathing stereotype: the department secretary without whom nothing got done and who knew all the department's workings. She knew all the idiosyncrasies of the faculty and steered students to this one or that depending on her judgment of the students' capabilities and personalities. Her wings seemed to have an endless extension, for she took the new faculty under them as well, helping them to adjust to the new surroundings and providing information about department history and regulations, as well as such practical matters as parking places. She could have advised the registrar on the several combinations of options for meeting the department's major and minor requirements.

Furthermore, she was an invaluable source of information to him as chair, and he knew it. She reminded him of the various deadlines of the college and university—deadlines for catalog information, for committee reports, for enrollment data, for library requests, and so on. She had seemingly endless counsel on which professor taught which courses best, and, as far as he had been able to tell, she was never wrong. In short, she was perfect. And that was her undoing.

It was her undoing because they lived in an imperfect world—in which the time of fiscal pressures and budget cutbacks had now arrived. He had been able to keep for her the special office she craved—office is the wrong word, but at least it had a door. He had been unable, however, to keep the third typist the whole department had come to enjoy. There was just not enough in the budget now that it had been reduced by 10 percent over the past year.

Although the budget had been reduced, the work load had not. The faculty was still generating research proposals and reports. Although no one had ever secured a grant large enough to support a full-time secretary, the little support they did secure seemed never to be enough. He certainly did not wish to discourage research or publication efforts, especially since he himself had emphasized its importance for promotion. In fact, he had his own small research project and depended on her for its record keeping. And, of course, the official requirements of the department office continued unabated.

As a result of these pressures, he had had to ask her to take on additional typing responsibilities for the department. He had asked her to develop a priority system for projects and had announced to the department that she would attempt to respond to some of their needs. He had been quite reluctant to take these steps, but an ugly scene at one of the department meetings had, he felt, left him no choice. Several faculty members—upset, he was sure, by the pressures and stress that a tightening budget inevitably brings—had suggested that with the loss of the third typist, it was time to relinquish his personal control of Miss Complait. Of course, he had never considered that he was in control of her, but in the confrontational atmosphere of the meeting he felt that he had no alternative but to agree to make her "more available."

Now she was in tears before him. She just did not have time, she said, to handle all of the demands upon her. The faculty seemed to consider that she was completely at their disposal and had no consideration for her work load. They all wanted projects completed by the end of the day and refused to listen to her side. The students were still coming to her for advice, and the faculty seemed to resent the time she was spending with them. Several had been quite rude, in fact, interrupting students to demand her attention. The respect she had always enjoyed in her position in the department seemed suddenly to have disappeared. And surely her job description did not include being at everyone's call and taking this abuse.

She had always taken pride, she continued, in being thorough and conscientious in her work as well as in being on top of department activities. Surely as the department secretary she should know what was going on. How else could she be helpful to him? Now, though, she felt she was losing control. He just had to do something, she concluded.

What should he do now?

Department secretaries can provide the chairperson with enormous assistance and, by the same token, they can create enormous difficulties. The following responses to this case study provide some suggestions both in proceeding and in clarifying roles.

Response #1

Without belaboring the psychodynamics of this case—who needs whom?—Miss Complait apparently likes her role *as it is.* The scope/focus was such that she was able to demonstrate (in her mind) that she was indispensable and certainly never expendable. She has carved out her turf and now when financial exigencies dictate a reshuffling of the deck she is playing "poor li'l ol' me." Her strong dedication to her existing job puts the chair in a double bind. Her track record of serving him well forces him to do things that could ultimately reduce his own comfort and, perhaps, status.

With the normal pressures to publish, the faculty is going to demand a change in the scope of her services. Besides, they have been able to function as prima donnas in the formerly fat system. Their needs and wants aren't likely to subside easily.

An efficiency study must be done to determine the college's and the department's needs and desires. The former denote what is necessary to survive and the latter serve as a "wouldn't it be nice if . . ." Perhaps a secretarial pool with work-study typists needs to be set up.

I do not think the chair needs to give Miss Complait to the department wolves, but he should indicate her role clearly to them. She serves the department in terms of *its* needs through the chair. Then the balance of time could be dispersed on an urgency and quality basis mediated by the chair (if necessary). Even the chair stands in line for nondepartmental or personal requests.

Check Miss Complait's job description. No need to cause problems with the classified workers' union or association. In addition, relieve her of her functions as an advice-giver (and sometimes quasi-counselor). Rotate an advisement pool of faculty or have them assigned to a cadre of advisees to handle on their own. Publish lists of course sequences and prerequisites in a student guide pamphlet. Have a work-study filter the phone calls to reduce interruptions for the secretary. Set up one night or one Saturday slot twice each semester just for advisement purposes (early and mid-semester—the latter for preregistration purposes for the next semester). (Fred E. Kirschner, Chairman, Counseling and Educational Psychology & Foundations, University of Nevada/Las Vegas.)

Response #2

We have all known the person described in "Department Secretary." The real problems in the case are not the ones related specifically to budget reductions; rather, they are associated with the department chairman's failure: (1) to establish a clearly understood job profile for each of the staff positions in the office, (2) to communicate to the staff what exactly is expected of them, and (3) to give this information to the faculty.

This department chairman must realize that he is responsible not only for the hiring of staff personnel but also for their organization as a functioning unit. The objectives of his department will not be met until the activities of the faculty and students are supported by a staff that works effectively together with executive leadership—the department chairman's leadership. As chairman, he is responsible for the direction and coordination of their effort. He must also develop a systematic check upon their performance and, when necessary, apply measures to minimize ineffective operation of the staff.

In this case, the department chairman must first develop a composite list of all responsibilities associated with each staff position in the office before the budget cutbacks occurred. Each of these responsibilities should then be listed according to priority by him. In turn, the responsibilities should be reassigned to the remaining staff positions in a manner that reflects the qualifications of the persons holding these staff appointments.

The chairman should then meet with Miss Complait. He should begin their conference by expressing his appreciation for everything she has done in the past to make the department function efficiently. While the chairman may wish to assure Miss Complait that he hopes she will be willing to continue her position, he must make it clear that, because of budget problems, some modifications will have to be made in the responsibilities that have been entrusted to her and to the other members of the staff in the past. He should then tactfully, but firmly, state his intention to provide executive leadership for the support staff as a whole, especially as it relates to the redefining of their responsibilities. He should then provide Miss Complait with some specific examples of modifications that will be made, such as:

1. Assigning *all* responsibilities for student advising to appropriate faculty members.

2. Providing specific guidelines for the faculty concerning the ways in which they will work with Miss Complait and other members of the staff in such areas as requests for typing of classroom materials and examinations; requests for copying services; requests related to grant proposals, reports, and record keeping.

Although a competent clerical staff usually performs its duties with little direct supervision, during the next several months the department chairman will need to provide close supervision of the staff, especially Miss Complait. During this time of adjustment to new ways of doing things, the chairman must make a special effort to maintain staff morale and to stimulate loyalty and understanding among the members of the staff. Taking the staff to lunch, involving them in department social activities, or establishing a special award for a specific staff accomplishment are some activities that may help in this area. (Donald E. McGlothlin, Chairman, Department of Music, University of Missouri/Columbia.)

Other troubling circumstances involving the department secretary can easily arise. For instance, consider the department secretary who brings his domestic quarrels to the office, telling them to any and all who are within earshot. Suppose further that the wife comes by to continue them. Similar situations can occur with other support staff, such as laboratory technicians. Consider also the staff member and the senior faculty member who are on a collision course. The chairperson witnesses a run-in. The staff person feels insulted and leaves in a huff, at which point the senior professor demands that she be fired for dereliction of duty. In each case the chairperson must respond with both delicacy and firmness.

Reduction of available resources frequently translates into reduction of support staff. The staff will feel overworked, as indeed they will be, at the same time that the faculty members will be frustrated by the lack of assistance. Dealing with the department morale difficulties this creates can be quite challenging. Perhaps of equal difficulty can be dealing with the loss of the competent secretary to the dean. The chairperson should also be alert to the issue of access to the secretary by teaching and research assistants. Policies should be developed and circulated to forestall problems.

CHAPTER SEVEN

Looking Toward the Future

CONSUMING THOUGH PRESENT PROBLEMS and concerns can be, it is necessary now and then to cast an eye toward the future. There is nothing I know of to suggest that the importance of either departments or of chairpersons will diminish in years to come. Doubtless a few institutions will continue to experiment with the idea of abolishing departments. More likely than not, however, they will find that programs and area concentrations will assume many of the characteristics of departments as basic curricular and accounting units—units charged organizationally with the development, preservation, and transmission of knowledge. Certainly, program or area directors and coordinators at such institutions look very much like chairpersons with another name.

The vast majority of institutions will continue with a departmental structure and will expect chairpersons to function as in the past, though with relatively restricted financial resources. The rich variety of specific traditions governing chairs will doubtless remain. Differences on the proper length of service will continue. One side will argue that all that a chair can do of a creative character will occur in three or four years. Others stress the importance of continuity in the office. Almost all agree that the stature of individual departments does much to determine the stature of the institution.

The Chairperson as Entrepreneur

Because of increasing financial constraints, many chairpersons will find themselves having to become entrepreneurs. For some, this will be an unaccustomed role. Most educators enter the profession because of the possibilities it offers for self-determination in teaching and research. For many, part of its attraction is also the absence of pressures to generate profits. Increasingly, however, chairpersons are realizing that departments are accounting as well as curricular units. A continued flow of institutional resources will often require concentrated effort on the part of the chair to justify them. The cumulative effect on the budget of various forces on the institution and department will demand that chairs develop at least some of the skills of the entrepreneur.

At a minimum, this will involve concern about levels of enrollment and retention. If the discipline is attracting increasing numbers of students, the chairperson will have to devise strategems to secure from the dean additional teaching staff. On the other hand, if the number of majors or of graduate students is falling, efforts must be initiated to enhance the department's attractiveness. If the department is primarily providing services to other departments, the chair must seek assurance that other departments and the dean completely understand and support this mission.

Exit interviews of students dropping out of department programs can provide helpful information about student perceptions of department strengths and weaknesses. The findings may relate to specific instructors as well as to curriculum offerings. Similar information can be secured from graduates of the department. In both cases the results can be put to good immediate use in aligning the department more closely to appropriate and legitimate student interests. Information gathered in this fashion together with that gleaned from developments in the discipline and needs in the surrounding community may also suggest the importance of developing some brand-new curricular thrusts. The willingness to collect such information and to act upon it is important for the integrity of the department and, in addition, can prove salutary for enrollments.

Improving the health of some departments will require the chairperson to explore ways of increasing external support. Departments with professional programs in particular come to mind. For example, those disciplines that provide graduates for area industries are in a good position to approach these industries for special support. Such support can take various forms, ranging from specific scholarships and donations of equipment, though special internship possibilities for both faculty and students, to supplements for faculty salaries. The last possibility should certainly be considered and explored by departments, such as engineering and accounting, where the salaries established by the marketplace are higher than what institutional resources can meet.

Special consulting arrangements with these industries may also be developed, with at least some of the revenues coming to the department. Individual faculty members may need to see some potential benefit before their enthusiasm can be aroused. In such cases, it is worthwhile to explore possible tax benefits to the individual of funds being channeled through the department. It is also possible for departments to provide special types of instruction for employees of area businesses, again with part of the revenues earmarked for department purposes.

In both cases, prior consultation and agreements with the dean are essential. In such discussions it is important to disclaim notions of empire building. Speak, rather, of building departmental strength or of serving the community. Be sure also to approach the dean for a return of a certain percentage of institutional indirect costs if your department has several research grants. It is not uncommon now for deans to make available such funds to reward department initiative. In fact, part of such funds can be earmarked for professional development expenses of those individuals responsible for securing the grants.

Do not overlook the possibility of using department alumni as an advisory body to the chair. Such bodies can provide helpful information on the adequacy of the curriculum and are also good for recruitment and placement of both students and faculty. In addition, they can be of considerable help in securing the kinds of external support mentioned above. Be aware, however, that such bodies can have wills of their own and can sometimes pressure the department in unwelcome ways.

The Chairperson as Creative Custodian of Standards

Many of the problems that chairpersons will have to address in coming years will be rooted in finances. But not all challenges will be financial in nature. In fact, many potential vexing problems stem directly from changes in social patterns and behaviors. For instance, as the pool of older, nontraditional, and part-time students increases relative to the population of eighteen- to twenty-four-year-olds, large adjustments in the attitudes and behaviors of many faculty members will be required. The precise requirements will differ from institution to institution, depending upon particular circumstances and traditions. And some of these adjustments will be automatic. Others, however, will be resisted, thereby posing difficult personnel situations for the chairperson.

Such matters as the need for changes in curricular presuppositions and adaptations in teaching techniques come directly to mind, but adjustments in research programs and activities may also prove difficult. Some professors will find disturbing the loss of deference, if not reverence, to which they had become accustomed. They may also find threatening the new breed of older students whose knowledge may well be equal or even superior to their own in the area of classroom inquiry. Certainly adjustments will have to be made in both course content and objectives. Such changes will need to be both encouraged and monitored by the chairperson.

The change in student populations will also bring the need for change in teaching schedules and instructional delivery mechanisms. Many colleges and universities are presently set up primarily for the convenience of the faculty. Monday-Wednesday-Friday teaching schedules leave generous amounts of time for research and consulting activities. But it may be that evening or weekend classes are what the institution and the students really need. Similarly, traditional curricula may need radical revision to meet changes in society or in the discipline itself. Yet most faculty are reluctant to change their established ways, and the chairperson will need to find ways to shift people's attitudes.

As the average student gets older, so, too, does the average faculty member. The chairperson will need to be alert to both the challenges and opportunities this creates. All the world must now know that American higher education is no longer a growth industry. The immobility in most academic disciplines may create general moods of depression, as teachers contemplate the lack of alternatives to what they may already have tired of. The dissatisfaction many feel may be compounded by their sense that a career in academia is a permanent commitment and that to contemplate alternative possibilities seriously is either disloyal or naive. Concern about financial security may also reduce the willingness to experiment with alternative career possibilities. The end result may easily be reduced professional luster and enthusiasm precisely at the stage when students and others expect wise and seasoned judgments and endorsements of the importance of the discipline.

Higher education has not done well so far in developing appropriate responses to this problem. It has been, and still is, true that faculty members generally enjoy remarkably free and unregimented work in an organizational environment traditionally characterized by substantial decentralization. People in other professions frequently enjoy no such benefits. And there are many with terminal degrees and splendid qualifications who would give all for a tenured slot. Still, the academic life can become cloying, and faculty members need the sense that there are alternatives.

The chairperson should be sensitive to these needs and be prepared to explore with faculty members ways in which new experiences can be devised or pursued. Such experiences can be short-term and temporary. For instance, faculty exchanges with departments at other institutions in the area can be a source of free but effective stimulation. Nearby institutions are especially attractive for such exchanges because they require none of the extensive logistical preparations that other types of exchanges can demand. The best arrangements seem to be the simplest ones, with both faculty members remaining on their home payrolls.

Short-term nonacademic experiences can be very valuable also. They can provide a refreshing change of pace for those who will return to the department afterward. They can also provide a nonthreatening trial experience for those who are considering possible longer term shifts. Given the logistical problems of moving, most opportunities will depend upon the local environment of the institution and the resources available in the community. In the smaller institutions, members of the board of trustees or regents can be helpful in identifying appropriate possibilities. Department alumni can also provide assistance.

Another very different set of problems can be seen developing from the tendency now of couples to delay starting a family until their late thirties. Not infrequently, these are also the same people who have traditionally been the leaders and the doers in department and college committees and activities. Thus, at the very time that institutions have become accustomed to relying on these people, they may become unavailable because of new family interests and responsibilities. Patterns of effective delegation and of informal institutional governance will be disrupted. New forms will have to be created. Certainly new problems will emerge in scheduling course and class assignments. The department's and institution's reward systems will have to be rethought. The case study "Scheduling Equity" will have fresh application!

Still another change in institutional behavior will have an impact on at least some chairpersons. I have in mind the increased turnover rate in the position of chairperson. Most departments will also continue to experience decreased opportunities for individual career mobility. As a result, a new chairperson may well find himself or herself with the special challenge of having within the department several prior chairs resentful of their current exclusion from power.

At almost any time, one can count on continuing conflicts between the research and teaching interests of individual faculty members and the broader needs and goals of the department. The department has to be more than the sum of its parts and it is the task of the chairperson to engineer ways in which this "more" can occur. Certainly there is no guarantee that allowing each department member unrestricted opportunity to pursue his or her special interests will promote the welfare of the whole. It is the risk-taking chairperson who will follow an undiluted Adam Smith concept of department affairs and governance. The trick is to discover or identify that viable middle path wherein the individual can find at least some of his or her interests advanced while also advancing department interests.

The values that the chairperson places on teaching and research and other activities will inevitably be reflected within the department, as faculty members respond to the signals provided by his or her salary and promotion recommendations. Nonfinancial incentives will be at play too, for people respond directly to such signs of encouragement as public and private words of appreciation and favorable course and classroom assignments. The tools for directing change are present, even if their effective application may take time.

The Chairperson as Politician

Let us look briefly at the relationships of the chairperson with the academic dean. It is difficult to overemphasize the importance of effective communications with the dean. To be effective, however, such communications must be appropriate. Supporting documentation must accompany all requests for resources or for activities out of the ordinary. Excessive documentation, however, can diminish rather than enhance the impression created. It suggests an inability to distinguish between the kernel and the chaff. Further, it implies that the chair and the department have no respect for the dean's time. There is a large role which intuition must play in such relationships. Knowing when something is enough and when it is too much is an art that must be cultivated. One must contrast the wisdom of the maxim "The squeaky wheel gets the grease" with that of "The honking goose gets shot." Timing can play an important role in such judgments.

Keep the dean informed about department activities outside the institution, particularly when these can affect other departments or institutional plans or projects. For instance, if the department is interested in soliciting support among area industries for special laboratory equipment, the dean should be given clear notice. The department should be sensitive to the possibility that someone in the administration will view such activity as an attempt to circumvent his or her office. As a result, such plans should be presented under the rubric of "marshalling support for the department," and efforts should be made to avoid perceptions of them as "end runs" around the administration.

Cultivating relationships with other departments is also important and can pay dividends down the road. Academic institutions are very political entities, and great skill can be required in protecting and developing department interests. For instance, it is important to secure the appointment of department faculty to key college and university committees. The objective is not merely to secure department interests narrowly defined, but also to provide wide understanding of the department's mission and accomplishments.

An especially exasperating issue for many chairpersons involves evaluation of their own performance as chairperson. Frequently, this issue can be resolved only at a higher level in the institution. Addressing it successfully can require considerable political savvy.

Procedures for evaluation of *faculty* will vary from institution to institution and often from department to department. However, there remains the traditional framework of instruction, research, and service. The institutional values associated with these categories may differ greatly, but there is at least some tacit understanding about organizational expectations and rewards. Likewise, there are many different methods and procedures for the evaluation of full-time *administrators*. One constant, however, is that at least a tacit understanding of shared expectations exists in the jointly negotiated job description. The reporting relationships reinforce these expectations.

The department chairperson, by contrast, can usually count on no such understandings, tacit or explicit. The department faculty may have totally unrealistic expectations of what the chair should be doing or can accomplish, and in any case will more often than not have no formal involvement in any substantive evaluation of the performance of the chairperson qua chairperson.

In fact, the normal state of affairs seems to be for the chairperson to be evaluated almost entirely by the same criteria that apply to full-time faculty members. Unable to compete equally because of reduced time available for research and instructional preparation, the chair can only suffer under these conditions. Institutions need to find ways to compensate for the disadvantage to which chairpersons are put under these circumstances. Those who are assistant or associate professors stand to lose the most by serving as chairperson, unless such service is realistically credited toward promotion. It is at this point that the institution is contributing to, and benefiting from, the ambiguity of the chairperson's position. It has a corresponding obligation to initiate equitable policies.

Such policies should also establish the criteria by which the accomplishments of chairs are to be identified and evaluated, thereby opening the door for realistic distribution of merit funds. To be sure, such determinations are not easy. However, recognition needs to be given to the chair who has defused a conflict-ridden department, or rejuvenated the instructional zip of a tired and inert faculty, or developed the research interests and accomplishments of a previously complacent body, or succeeded in bringing the department to meet a changed clientele and mission.

The Satisfactions of the Position

Little direct attention has been given yet to the question of why department chairs serve or the rewards and satisfaction they might find in serving. Indeed, the number of challenging, if not sometimes almost unanswerable, case studies that have been presented here may have created the impression that the position at best is tolerable and at worst a punishment for previous high-order sins. In fact, however, reports suggest otherwise. In conducting numerous workshops for chairpersons from all types of institutions and from all regions of the country, I have had the opportunity to inquire directly about reasons why the position was accepted and the kinds of satisfactions found in the job. Even though the typical responsibilities of the position seem to be at odds with the attractions of the professoriate, the overwhelming number of participants in these workshops reported finding large measures of satisfaction in serving as chair.

Despite the deadlines, budget demands, and other forms of administrative accountability that go with the job of chair but not with that of professor, more than 80 percent of the respondents indicated large satisfaction in the job. The specific question to which they responded was whether or not they would serve another term if requested. Only three groups deviated from this response. The first was of chairpersons at institutions with immediate and severe financial difficulties. The second was of those who had already served as chair for several years, usually more than ten. The third group was composed of those individuals who were concerned about their own loss of research productivity.

Fully 80 percent indicated that they would gladly serve longer. Among the favors cited in support of their willingness was the opportunity the position provided to exercise influence over the department's mission and the curriculum. The correction of existing programs figured largely as did the possibility of instituting new programs. Many cited the attractiveness of being able to support individuals who had contributed significantly to the department's or institution's activities and objectives. Others mentioned the continuing need for a challenge beyond the familiar responsibilities of teaching and research.

There does come a point, however, when one has run through his or her effectiveness. Leadership has to be highly situational—responsive to the cycles and rhythms of the organization. Thresholds of department morale and receptiveness to innovation will vary according to recent events but are extremely important in establishing what a chairperson can easily accomplish. Individuals need to be alert to such facts of life. Unfortunately, too many people reach the point of ineffectiveness before they realize they are headed in that direction. Given the proper framework, however, the position can be very satisfying. Certainly it is a key to the success of the institution.

Suggested Readings

ANDERSON, G. LESTER. "Organizational Diversity." In *New Directions for Institutional Research: Examining Departmental Management*, edited by John C. Smart and James R. Montgomery. San Francisco: Jossey-Bass, 1976.

ATWELL, ROBERT H., and GREEN, MADELEINE F., eds. *New Directions for Higher Education: Academic Leaders as Managers*. San Francisco: Jossey-Bass, 1981.

BARE, ALAN C. "The Study of Academic Department Performance." *Research in Higher Education*, 1980, 12(1):3–22.

BENNETT, JOHN B. "A Chairperson's Notes to the Dean." *AAHE Bulletin*, June 1982, pp. 15–16.

———. "Ambiguity and Abrupt Transitions in the Department Chairperson's Role." *Educational Record*, Fall 1982, pp. 53–56.

———. "Inside a Department Chairperson." *AGB Reports*, May/June 1982, pp. 39–42.

BERGMANN, THOMAS J., and O'MALLEY, JOHN T. "The Department Chairperson in Campus Governance." *The Journal of College and University Personnel Association*, Fall 1979, pp. 7–17.

BERGQUIST, WILLIAM H.; PHILIPS, STEVEN R.; and QUEHL, GARY H. *A Handbook for Faculty Development.* Washington, D.C.: Council for the Advancement of Small Colleges, 1975.

BOOTH, DAVID B. "The Department Chair: Professional Development and Role Conflict." AAHE-ERIC Higher Education Research Report 10, 1982. Washington, D.C.: American Association for Higher Education, 1982.

——. "Institutional and Disciplinary Ideas for Development." *Educational Record,* Winter 1977, pp. 83–90.

BRANN, JAMES, and EMMET, THOMAS A., eds. *The Academic Department or Division Chairman: A Complex Role.* Detroit: Balamp, 1972.

BUHL, LANCE C., and GREENFIELD, ADELE. "Contracting for Professional Development in Academe." *Educational Record,* Spring 1975, pp. 111–121.

CENTRA, JOHN A. *Determining Faculty Effectiveness: Assessing Teaching, Research and Service for Personnel Decisions and Improvement.* San Francisco: Jossey-Bass, 1980.

DRESSEL, PAUL L. *Handbook of Academic Evaluation: Assessing Instructional Effectiveness, Student Progress, and Professional Performance for Decision-Making in Higher Education.* San Francisco: Jossey-Bass, 1976.

——; JOHNSON, F. CRAIG; and MARCUS, PHILIP M. *The Confidence Crisis: An Analysis of University Departments.* San Francisco: Jossey-Bass, 1970.

EBLE, KENNETH E. "What to Say about Teaching at Tenure Time." *ADE Bulletin,* May 1978, pp. 30–33.

EHRLE, ELWOOD B. "Selection and Evaluation of Department Chairmen." *Educational Record,* Winter 1975, pp. 28–38.

——, and EARLEY, JANE F. "The Effect of Collective Bargaining on Departmental Chairpersons and Deans." *Educational Record,* 1976, 57(3):149–154.

FISHER, CHARLES F. "Being There Vicariously by Case Studies." In *On College Teaching,* edited by Ohmer Milton and Associates. San Francisco: Jossey-Bass, 1978.

FURNISS, W. TODD. *Reshaping Faculty Careers.* Washington, D.C.: American Council on Education, 1981.

GAFF, JERRY G. "Current Issues in Faculty Development." *Liberal Education,* December 1977, pp. 511–519.

————. *Toward Faculty Renewal: Advances in Faculty, Instructional, and Organizational Development.* San Francisco: Jossey-Bass, 1975.

HOBBS, WALTER C. "Academic Departments and the Law." In *Examining Departmental Management,* edited by JOHN C. SMART AND JAMES R. MONTGOMERY. San Francisco:Jossey-Bass, 1976.

LEVINE, ARTHUR. *Why Innovation Fails: The Institutionalization and Termination of Innovation in Higher Education.* Albany, N.Y.: State University of New York Press, 1981.

LINDQUIST, JACK. *Strategies for Change: Academic Innovation and Adaptive Development.* Washington, D.C.: Council for the Advancement of Small Colleges, 1980.

MAGUIRE, JOHN DAVID. "Can Change Be Institutionalized? How?" *Liberal Education,* 1977, 63:584–589.

McHENRY, DEAN E., and ASSOCIATES. *Academic Departments: Problems, Variations, and Alternatives.* San Francisco: Jossey-Bass, 1977.

McKEACHIE, WILBERT J. "Memo to New Department Chairmen." *Educational Record,* Spring 1968, pp. 221–227.

NEUMANN, YORAM, and BORIS, STEVEN B. "Paradigm Development and Leadership Style of University Department Chairpersons." *Research in Higher Education,* 1978, 9(4).

REHNKE, MARY ANN. "A Primer for Department Chairpersons." *AAHE Bulletin,* June 1982, pp. 13–15.

SCOTT, ROBERT A. "Portrait of a Department Chairperson." *AAHE Bulletin,* February 1981, pp. 1, 3–6.

SELDIN, PETER. *Successful Faculty Evaluation Programs: A Practical Guide to Improve Faculty Performance and Promotion/Tenure Decisions.* New York: Coventry Press, 1980.

TUCKER, ALLAN. *Chairing the Academic Department.* Washington, D.C.: American Council on Education, 1981.

WALKER, DONALD E. *The Effective Administrator: A Practical Approach to Problem Solving, Decision Making and Campus Leadership.* San Francisco: Jossey-Bass, 1979.

WALTZER, HERBERT. *The Job of the Academic Department Chairman.* Washington, D.C.: American Council on Education, 1975.

Index